VANISHING
FATHERS

The ripple effect on tomorrow's generation

VANISHING
FATHERS

The ripple effect on tomorrow's generation

JAMIE TRUMAN

Truman Charities

Truman Charities

Bethesda, Maryland
https://www.trumancharities.com
info@trumancharities.com

ISBN: 979-8-9900328-0-4 (paperback)
ISBN: 979-8-9900328-1-1 (hardcover)
ISBN: 979-8-9900328-2-8 (e-book)
Library of Congress Control Number: 2024902419

Edited by Melanie Mulhall, Dragonheart
Design by Nick Zelinger, NZ Graphics
Cover photo by Heather Dearborn

First Edition
Printed in the United States of America

To my loving husband, Jerry, and three beautiful boys, Zack, Dominic, and Antonio.

Contents

Foreword

I have always believed that if you are in constant search for inspiration, not only will you find it, you will meet inspirational people with incredible stories that can have profound effects on your life and on the lives of so many other people. This is how my journey has intersected with Jamie Truman.

At the age of seventeen, I was a nationally ranked quarterback coming out of DeMatha Catholic High School—generally ranked somewhere between number two and number five in the nation behind some guy named Peyton Manning. Just when I thought my life's dream to play football in college was unfolding before my eyes, I broke my neck in a diving accident at the beach prior to my senior year of high school. It left me paralyzed from a spinal cord injury and confined to a wheelchair as a quadriplegic. I met Jerry Truman and his brother, Matt, while we were all students at DeMatha in the early '90s. They witnessed those early days of my journey.

Jerry and I have been able to extend our friendship throughout the last three decades, during which we both have lived in the Maryland suburbs of the Washington metropolitan area. That began when we were at the University of Maryland in our twenties and thirties and found ourselves in one or another of the fine local drinking establishments. We not only shared a friendship but also great admiration for one another as we both matured and navigated life, careers, marriage, and kids.

For twenty-two years I was a color analyst covering University of Maryland football games on the radio alongside Johnny Holliday. I also got my law degree from Georgetown University, worked as a lawyer, and became a motivational speaker. During this time, Jerry was building his own successful career as a financial advisor and all the while, was getting involved in philanthropy. I had great admiration for his enthusiasm to help others and raise money for causes. Then Jamie and Jerry cofounded Truman Charities and have since raised close to two million dollars for various causes.

As if that weren't enough inspiration, I then became aware of Jamie's own personal project. Through her podcast, as well as her reflections on her personal experience and her work with charities, she found a common denominator in the impact fathers can have—both good and bad—on the lives of their children: A father's presence or absence impacts the lives of their children, along with the quality of their involvement. Her challenges with her father sparked her research into this phenomenon, and she was able to connect with many inspirational people who have overcome their own challenges with an absent or abusive father. The people she has interviewed and included in this book have incredible stories that are filled with inspiration. Jamie's own experiences add a personal touch to the inspirational journeys shared in this book.

When I speak, I tell my audiences that the most common question I get is, "Tim, how do you do it?" Many people look at my situation and think to themselves that they could not do what I have done following my accident if it were them. We have all looked at someone going through a challenging adversity and couldn't imagine how we would respond or if we would respond the way that person did. As an inspirational speaker, I try to relay to my audience that they could indeed do it. We all have the capacity to overcome any adversity. I use my story and that of others to provide examples for people to draw that inspiration from. In *Vanishing Fathers,* Jamie's story and those of others demonstrate that point. We can achieve great success in spite of challenging circumstances.

As someone with a great father who has been there with me and who is one of the most supportive and important people in helping me face my adversity, I look at the subjects of this book, as well as Jamie, and cannot help but wonder how they have done it without the love and support from their fathers. They each provide me with inspiration to incorporate into my own journey and my quest to achieve success and happiness despite any adversity that tries to get in my way.

Thank you, Jamie, for letting me be a part of your journey and for bringing this collection of inspirational people into my life through this book. I am confident that everyone who reads it will draw the same inspiration and apply it to their own lives and circumstances regardless of the relationship they have with their own father. I am so lucky that my constant search for inspiration has not only been rewarded through the examples of inspirational people like those you highlight in this book, but has also connected me to good people like you and Jerry. Congratulations on a great book I know everyone will enjoy!

Tim Strachan
February 2024

Preface

Iheard my husband and three boys laughing as they wrestled in the family room, and a broad smile crossed my face. I couldn't imagine a more vivid demonstration of the bond between fathers and sons and how the role of a man is so significant in family life.

It was a stark contrast to a scene that played out on my television screen in which a crowd of women cheered a speaker who declared, "Men are disposable. Society does not need men to thrive. We are better off without them."

What nonsense, I thought. Why would anyone think men have a negative impact on society? Isn't the value of strong men and loving, involved fathers obvious? I knew from my own childhood how devastating it can be without a father in your life because mine was gripped by a drug addiction. I also saw the effects on children of not having a father figure from my charitable work and from hosting a podcast.

In 2010, my husband Jerry and I cofounded a volunteer-based organization, Truman Charities, which hosts several events a year for different nonprofits. Then in April of 2021, I created the Truman Charities podcast and have interviewed numerous nonprofit founders. To my surprise, I have found that a major underlying factor in the lives of individuals who suffered poverty, homelessness, addiction, and incarceration was that they grew up in fatherless homes.

Without the guiding hand of a good father, many children are more likely to fail academically and socially, and worse still, go off the rails and be easy prey for drugs pushers and sex traffickers.

Deciding to delve further into this important topic, I dug through a wide range of studies and interviewed men and women from different ethnicities and backgrounds to put a personal face to this national tragedy. What kinds of challenges did they face with an abusive or absent father? How did they manage to overcome them? What did they learn? I desperately wanted to find answers, not only to show my sons how valuable they are in society but also to give hope to young men who may feel lost and unsure how to navigate their way into adulthood.

I started close to home with my own story and that of my brother from another father, as well as my husband and my father-in-law. The stories that follow include the lives of people who were driven to attempt suicide, fell into drug addiction, and coped with the death of a father. They also include the stories of a man whose early years were spent in a religious cult due to a brainwashed father and two women who fell victim to sex traffickers.

All the stories highlight the benefits of an involved father and the potential dangers when a father is not in the lives of their children. My goal is to emphasize the value of father-hood to young men, inspire them to actively participate in raising their sons and daughters, and experience the kind of joy I heard in my husband's voice as he played with our sons. That day spoke to me. It motivated me to actively do whatever I can to eliminate the epidemic of vanishing fathers.

Chapter 1

The Fatherhood Factor

You've certainly heard the expression "Like father, like son." As with many sayings, it has entered the popular lexicon because it rings true. The presence or absence of a father in the home has a massive impact, especially on boys.

According to a report by the US Department of Health and Human Services, it used to be the case that, "Too many fathers become convinced that they are simply an extra set of hands to help around the house, rather than irreplaceable to their children."

Whether or not many fathers still believe that, it couldn't be further from the truth. Extensive research has highlighted both the positives of a father's involvement and the negatives when a father is either absent or abusive.

Top researcher David Popenoe, professor of sociology emeritus and codirector of The National Marriage Project at Rutgers University, says, "Based on the evidence, a strong case can be made that paternal deprivation, in the form of the physical, economic, and emotional unavailability of fathers to their children, has become the most prevalent form of child maltreatment today. Fathers are vanishing from family life and only mothers are left to care about the children. And mothers are not enough."

Leading expert and author on the issue, Henry B. Biller, professor of psychology at the University of Rhode Island, makes the case that nothing is more important than the quality of the father-child relationship. He says it is the single variable that is most consistently linked to positive life outcomes.

The presence of a father has proven to be beneficial from the moment of birth. Swedish researchers found that babies who experienced skin-to-skin contact with their fathers cried less, calmed quicker, and fell asleep faster. The beneficial impact of loving and involved dads begins but certainly doesn't end in the nursery. It continues throughout childhood as kids develop emotionally, physically, and intellectually. Even infants as young as five months score higher on measures of cognitive development if they have highly involved fathers who take part in play and caregiving activities.

The more time fathers spend with their babies, the better they understand their cues. And the better they understand their cues, the stronger the possibility for the forging of a healthy attachment. When fathers are engaged in taking care of their infants, the positive results are clear. Babies become more resilient and curious and are more confident to branch out and explore.

One study that looked at three-year-olds found that when fathers participated in their childcare, their social development benefited. In another study, one exploring empathy in grade school children, those who'd had secure attachments to their fathers as babies were better able to identify other children's feelings and take steps to make them feel better.

One six-year study discovered that paternal (but not maternal) warmth had a significant long-term effect in shaping adolescents' attitudes toward such social issues as marriage, divorce, sex roles, child support, welfare, and teen-age childbearing. More specifically, the warmer the father's behavior and the more the adolescents participated in family decision making, the more they adopted their parents' values as their own.

Of course, there are also ways in which males interact with sons that females don't. Fathers engage in more physical, rough-and-tumble, and idiosyncratic play than mothers do. And fathers are more likely than mothers to encourage children's competitiveness, independence, and risk-taking such as carrying scissors, crossing the street, or bathing themselves. As a result, their children develop belief in their abilities and their thinking skills improve, according to research by Ronald P. Rohner of the University of Connecticut and Robert A. Veneziano of Western Connecticut State University.

Kids with involved fathers report that they're happier and less anxious. They have better relationships and less conflict with their siblings and peers. They perform better across the spectrum of educational competence, from getting better grades to being more motivated and placing a higher value on education.

Another important link to consider is economics. Fathers who are more involved with their children are also more likely to provide for them financially, and children who are better off financially do better in school.

One thing is certain: Fathers who spend a lot of time helping their children with their studies increase the quality of their children's learning. They can also help their children's thinking skills—and their success later in life—by being involved with their social, fitness, and sports activities. In adolescence, avoiding negative behaviors becomes even more important since the stakes can be higher, and a close relationship with a father can help adolescents stay on the right track.

Father-child relationships even affect a child's future marriage. Children who have involved fathers are more likely as adults to have long-term, successful marriages and are less likely to divorce. When a man is both a nurturing parent and supportive husband, the evidence is clear that the wife becomes a more effective parent, and when both parents are warm and loving, children are major beneficiaries.

The Downside

According to the US Census Bureau, in 2023 some 15.08 million children lived in a home without the benefit of a biological, step, or adoptive father. That's one out of every five. And it's the highest rate in the world—almost three times the global average according to the Pew Research Center. Let's look at some statistics that help paint the full picture.

- Eighty-four percent of homeless families are headed by women, according to the American College of Gynecologists and Obstetricians.

- Seventy-one percent of children who abuse substances are from fatherless homes, according to the nonprofit National Center for Fathering.

- In a study of fifty-six school shootings, a shocking 82 percent of the shooters grew up in either an unstable family environment or without both biological parents together, according to the Rand Corporation.

As Clare Morell, senior policy analyst at the Ethics and Public Policy Center, puts it, "Fathers are essential to the flourishing of our country. Having a father in the home dramatically reduces a myriad of harms." But she also points out that the absence of father is a crisis in the US. "Consequently," she says, "there is a 'father factor' in nearly all social ills facing America today."

It's a situation that has changed dramatically over the years. Among children who were part of the post-war generation (baby boomers), 87.7 percent grew up with two biological parents who were married to each other. Today only 68.1 percent will spend their entire childhood in an intact family.

"The evidence is overwhelming: Children from single-parent homes have more behavioral problems, are more likely to get in trouble in school or with the law, achieve lower levels of education and tend to earn lower incomes in adulthood. Boys from homes without dads present are particularly prone to getting in trouble in school or with the law," says Melissa S. Kearney, author of *The Two-Parent Privilege: How Americans Stopped Getting Married and Started Falling Behind* in a *New York Times* guest essay.

Research shows that parental divorce is worse for a child than when the father dies or is killed. Sara McLanahan and

Gary Sandefur, authors of *Growing Up with a Single Parent,* say, "When a child's father dies or is killed, children fare somewhat better than when there is no father in their life because of divorce. They don't do as well as those children fortunate enough to have both parents present but they don't feel deliberately abandoned."

Studies going back decades show that negative or hostile relationships with fathers can result in negative social behavior and difficult peer relationships. When fathers are absent, according to work published by the Centre for Families, Work and Well-Being, "Boys, on average, are more likely to be more unhappy, sad, depressed, dependent, and hyperactive. Girls . . . are more likely to become overly dependent and have internalizing problems such as anxiety and depression."

From the educational standpoint, studies have shown that students whose fathers are absent from the home are twice as likely to repeat a grade, and in turn, poor academic performance increases the risk of delinquency. And according to researchers Sheila Fitzgerald Krein and Andrea H. Beller, 71 percent of high school dropouts have minimal or no father involvement.

Why is that? Children growing up in fatherless homes may lack the guidance, discipline, and emotional support that a father provides. This could have a domino effect, leading to difficulty forming positive relationships and the likelihood of involvement in criminal activity. There are statistics to validate this observation. US Department of Justice reports have found that 70 percent of juveniles in state operated institutions have no father in the household.

Sad to say, around 90 percent of runaways and homeless youths come from fatherless homes, and children from father-absent homes are more likely to commit a range of crimes from shoplifting to murder. Every 1 percent increase in fatherlessness in a neighborhood predicts a 3 percent increase in adolescent violence, according to one report.

Among the most dramatic impacts reported by the Center for Successful Fathering is that the chance a young male will get involved in criminal activity triples if he is raised without a father. Shockingly, 80 percent of rapists assessed as raping out of anger and rage and 72 percent of murderers grew up without a father in the home. One study of 835 juvenile male inmates found that those from father-absent homes were 279 percent more likely to carry guns and deal drugs than peers who lived with their fathers. Princeton University research discovered that boys are significantly more likely to end up in jail or prison by the time they turn thirty if they are raised by a single mother.

It's a self-perpetuating scenario. Men who are raised without fathers are more apt to become absent fathers themselves. Like father, like son.

No wonder the National Center for Fathering, which was created in response to the social and economic impact of fatherlessness in America, says, "If it were classified as a disease, fatherlessness would be an epidemic worthy of attention as a national emergency."

The epidemic of non-father homes is a crisis for the country. And it is why one of the ways I address these issues is with stories of real people with vastly different experiences, good and bad, starting with my own.

My Story

Young girls depend on their fathers for security and emotional support. A father shows his daughter what a good relationship with a man is like. If a father is loving and gentle, his daughter will look for those qualities in men when she's old enough to begin dating. If a father is strong and valiant, she will relate closely to men of the same character. The presence of a father in a girl's home can greatly influence her growth, development, and overall well-being.

This may sound like common sense, but it is substantiated by numerous scientific studies and reports. For instance, a review of twenty-four studies published in *Acta Paediatrica* found that girls with involved fathers tend to perform better academically, including having higher grades, higher test scores, and increased likelihood of completing college. They're also more likely to have a positive body image and sense of self-worth.

Research published in the *Journal of Adolescence* found similarly better academic performance for girls who have an involved father and notes they also become assertive without being aggressive and have more confidence in relationships. Daughters who have close relationships with their dads have higher grade point averages than those without that strong connection.

Studies also show that strong and warm father-daughter relationships ward off depression and anxiety in teenage years and beyond, and the daughter is less likely to suffer eating disorders.

Emotionally, good daughter-dad relationships lead to girls developing intimate and fulfilling relationships with boyfriends and future husbands. "The daughter who has a fulfilling relationship with her father is usually more trusting, more secure and more satisfied in her romantic relationships than the daughter with a troubled or distant relationship with her dad," said Linda Neilson, a professor of psychology at Wake Forest University and an expert in father-daughter relationships. "Women who grow up with meaningful, comfortable, conversational relationships with their dads make better choices in who they date, sleep with, and marry." It's true, she says, whether parents are divorced or married.

One study showed that fathers are more likely than mothers to give daughters the opportunity to be more adventurous. Dads were more willing, for instance, to let their three- and four-year-old daughters play on a five-foot-high catwalk or walk across a three-foot-high beam. And it's usually dads who encourage their girls to pursue sports.

Improved relationships were also emphasized in a US Department of Health and Human Services report. "Girls with involved, respectful fathers see how they should expect men to treat them and are less likely to become involved in violent or unhealthy relationships."

The downsides of daughters not having a father participating in their lives are numerous, according to the Rochester Area Fatherhood Network. It says 53 percent are more likely to marry as teenagers, 71 percent are more likely to have children as teenagers, and 92 percent are more likely to get divorced. A University of Arizona study found that about one-third of girls whose fathers left the home before they reached six became pregnant as teenagers versus no more than 5 percent of girls whose fathers were a constant in their lives. Other studies indicate teenage girls without involved dads are twice as likely to engage in sex at an earlier age and seven times more likely to get pregnant. Women whose fathers were absent when they were children are more likely to have children with men who become absent partners.

Without a father figure in their lives, girls may lack the emotional support and guidance needed to develop a strong sense of self-worth and make healthy choices. This can leave them vulnerable to exploitation by sex traffickers. According to The Institute for Shelter Care, 70 percent of exploited women grew up without a father in the home.

I know all too well the impact of growing up without a father as a positive role model. And apart from the research I have done, it gives me some authority to speak on the subject.

My Story

My father was a kind man with a wonderful sense of humor. I have fond memories of going to his house in New Jersey in the summer, getting ice cream, and visiting the water park. Dad called me Jamesly, and he always said, "Jamesly, you are the most beautiful girl in the whole world." Unfortunately, these memories are intertwined with feelings of abandonment, resentment, and distrust caused by his alcohol and drug abuse. His substance abuse eventually killed him.

My mother and father, Joanne and Dave, met when they were in ninth grade and only fifteen years old. They started dating the following year, shortly after Dad dropped out of school and went to work to help his family. Although he didn't have much of an education and never graduated, he did learn about alcohol at a young age. He told me his dad took him to a bar for a drink when he was only thirteen.

My parents divorced when I was very young because of Dad's issues with alcohol. He'd often go on benders for several days, and my mother would have no idea where he was. I don't remember them living together with me and my two older brothers, Michael and DJ. Dad was often away from home. He had his own construction business working in places like Philadelphia, New York, and New Jersey, and he would be gone for a week or two at a time. Mom told me she loved him greatly, but it was actually more difficult when he was home than when he was away.

Dad was like a lot of alcoholics. He would be productive for a while, fall off the wagon, and climb back on. When I was little, we'd see him at my aunt's or grandmother's house on holidays and would have a great time. He was easy to love. He played with us, but it was more like having a fun uncle than a dad.

When I was three years old, I was diagnosed with a rare condition, precocious puberty. It's like having a faucet of hormones turned on full blast, and you have your first period around the age of five. It comes with a lot of side effects and social issues. If left untreated, you only grow to the height of an average five-year-old. When they worked out that I had precocious puberty, they told Mom of a new experimental drug she would have to get via Johns Hopkins. Typically, insurance didn't cover experimental drugs, and it was expensive. We had little money. Mom was barely making ends meet trying to go to school and work.

When I was four or five, I got out of bed one night and heard Mom on the phone with Dad, yelling and crying. I was really confused. I didn't understand why she was so mad at him, but that conversation stuck in my head. I found out much later that she was begging him to help pay for my medication that month and he wouldn't. My father never once pitched in for the cost of my medication. If it weren't for the generosity of my grandmother and eventually my stepfather, I might not have received the medication I desperately needed. I have so much respect for my mom because if it had been left to my dad, I would have had an extremely difficult life. But I think he didn't understand the responsibilities involved in raising kids because of his addiction.

I grew up in a house in a nice suburb of Annapolis where it was unheard of to have a dad in jail, but my dad was in and out of jail the majority of my life. Divorce wasn't uncommon, but mostly parents had fifty-fifty custody and you'd see dads at their kids' games. Of my two best friends, one set of parents are still together, and while the other's parents divorced, I was always jealous because my friend's dad doted on her. It made me realize that what I had wasn't normal.

Despite the situation, Mom would never say anything bad about Dad.

One incident that had a significant impact on me happened when my dad was due to take me for the weekend. It was special because for once, my two older brothers would not be with us. I sat outside the front door clutching my purple teddy bear duffle bag, eagerly waiting for him to pick me up. The hours ticked by. I would not go inside. Mom kept saying maybe he was sick. There was nothing for me to do but stare at the sky, and I sat there for hours until it got so late I had to go in. As an adult, I look back and think how sad it was for a young child to sit there anxiously waiting for so long while her mom made excuses for her delinquent dad.

I was eight or nine when I realized he was an addict. He'd remarried by this time, had twin boys, a beautiful home, and was running his own construction company. He picked up my two brothers and me to spend a week's vacation with them. As we drove along the freeway, he told us he needed something and got off at an exit. Cars beeped their horns like crazy as we drove the wrong way before pulling into a gas station. My brothers and I stood outside the car waiting for him, and a woman came up screaming, "Don't get back in the car. Don't get back in the car."

I challenged her. "What's wrong with you? That's my dad. What are you talking about?"

The woman insisted, "He's on something. He's completely wasted."

"You're crazy. He's fine," I claimed with the certainty of a know-nothing child. "He's just tired."

Dad had kept saying he was tired because he'd worked all day. The people at the gas station knew better and called the police. Dad was arrested. When our stepmom picked us up, she also insisted he was simply tired and pleaded, "Please don't tell your mom." It didn't make sense to me. I knew no one got arrested for being tired. As young as I was, that was when I realized he had a problem. Thank God for the lady at the gas station.

Directly after that incident, Dad and his new family moved from New Jersey to my stepmother's father's house in Maryland, ostensibly to take care of him. But he wasn't frail or ninety years old, and when we visited, he actually helped take care of us. I was at the age when you understand that parents didn't always tell the truth. Until then, you believe anything that comes out of their mouths. You're easy to manipulate— little sponges who soak up whatever your parents say.

I must have been in sixth or seventh grade when we got some blunt truth from Mom. She took us three kids to a little Chinese restaurant near our home and broke the news this way: "I have to tell you something. When you see your father, you have to understand something about him. He's HIV positive."

I wasn't quite sure what that meant. I'd heard about it on TV and I knew it was a disease. I knew people died. My mom was a nurse and explained it as best she could. I discovered that not only did my dad drink a lot, he'd also started doing drugs. He was on heroin. He'd been on heroin when that episode in the car happened.

We were warned to protect ourselves around him. Avoid razors. That kind of thing. I became obsessed with the diagnosis. It shaped a lot of my life because I was terrified of it. When I got older and began dating, I was scared to be intimate with anyone because I thought I could die from it.

After my dad got the diagnosis, he went into a nosedive. He thought his life was over and continued to do drugs. Of course, this was back in the nineties before innovative drugs helped people with HIV live productive and healthy lives. When I visited him, I was hyperaware of everything. Toward the end of his life, he had scabs that bled a lot. He looked like a skeleton, frail and helpless, nothing like the big, burly Southern guy I knew as a child who loved his Ford pickup truck and country music. It was sad. I saw his imperfections and I was devastated. I knew the end was coming.

I spent a lot more time with him toward the end, but I didn't feel comfortable and left when some of his buddies stopped by because I knew those were the friends he did drugs with. You could see in his eyes that he had given up. He wanted to die. He didn't care because he didn't feel that his life had any meaning. One night he took drugs and his body just couldn't take it. And that was the end. The grief was intense. When it comes to your parents, it doesn't matter what they've done. They still gave you life.

A couple of days after he passed, I was cleaning out his house and found a picture of my cousin, who had been one of my best friends in our younger days. Sadly, she'd also become hooked on heroin, got involved with a pimp, and become a prostitute. I asked my grandma what had happened to her and learned that she was dead. She'd been found naked in an abandoned car. It was surmised she'd been with a client, but my grandma didn't know if she'd overdosed or if there was foul play. My cousin was nineteen. I was angry. Why did she and my dad have to end up like that?

At the funeral home with my mother and DJ, I kissed my father on his forehead and said goodbye. He felt cold and hard. I didn't cry, but seeing my father in a coffin didn't seem real. It was like I was watching a movie.

I did get upset when I realized we could not afford to grant his wish to be buried. He always said he did not want to be cremated, but my brother and I were broke college kids. I had no idea how we were going to pay for a cremation, let alone a burial. Fortunately, my loving grandmother (on my mother's side) who'd always been so kind to my father and helped take care of him from time to time since he was a fifteen-year-old kid, paid for the cremation and memorial service. I have always been blessed to have her in my life.

Dad's memorial service was sad, in part because almost no one from his side of the family showed up. One of my cousins and her boyfriend were high on heroin and caused more of a scene than anything else. When the music began, I cried for the first time.

Our dad was such a wonderful man with so much potential, but addiction took over his life and ultimately took his life. It left me with the strong conviction that the only way to honor him would be to never become addicted to alcohol or drugs and to provide children of my own with opportunities he never had.

I have an addictive personality, which comes from my father's side of the family. I have to be honest about it and I have to fight it. When I was younger, I'd drink to an extreme. In my late teens I smoked a pack of cigarettes a day. When I stopped smoking, I switched to drinking lots of water, partly to satisfy the hand to mouth need. My brain has to work by substituting a bad habit with a good habit.

After my father's passing, I had to do something to alleviate the grief. The solution I came up with might seem dramatic: It was to run a marathon and raise funds for the Whitman-Walker Clinic, which helped people with HIV/AIDS. I wasn't a runner. I probably hadn't run any further than three times around the cul-de-sac. On my first training run, I fell down and doubted the wisdom of my decision, but I persevered and threw myself into training. I found that running was a cathartic experience. And the release of endorphins gave me the kind of high I needed, and that's my addiction. If I go two days without sweating, my mood changes for the worse.

After Dad's death, I grew up quickly. I waited tables during the day while I went to college in the evenings and started a fitness business. The mistake I made was to date people who embodied the negative attributes of either my dad or stepdad—men with traits I would never want in a husband. The men I dated were either verbally abusive while drinking or emotionally unavailable. As you can imagine, those relationships did not end very well. Then I asked myself what on earth am I doing. I was in very bad relationships, and the common denominator was me. It was not their fault. I chose to date those men.

My next course of action was one of the best things I've ever done, and I encourage anyone who is looking for a partner to do the same. I wrote down the exact attributes I wanted in a partner. They needed to be loyal, faithful, kind, generous, financially stable, and filled with purpose. Then I realized that to find that person, I had to be that person. I had to be accountable for and to myself. I couldn't expect someone to treat me well and not yell at me if I was verbally abusive to them. I couldn't expect someone to be financially stable if I was in complete disarray and didn't have my life together.

I worked hard and thanked God for my mom, who supported me every way possible. She let me move back home and sleep on her couch when I was in my mid-twenties. And we made it work. I built two very successful businesses, one in fitness and the other in marketing, and I worked like crazy seven days a week. With the kind of work ethic I inherited from my dad, I was out in the streets posting signs for boot camps at 2:00 a.m. I got myself completely out of debt.

I always wanted to be like my mom's side of the family, who were all well-educated. I especially wanted to be like DJ, who would take forty-five minutes to study for a test and ace it, or like Michael, who got straight As. I always struggled to take tests and never flourished in school. But as I got older, I realized you have to be thankful for the gifts you are given, and I was blessed with my father's savvy business sense.

I was hell-bent on becoming the person I had written down, and I was determined to be a better friend to my friends. I knew I would never find a good husband and bring children into the world if I didn't change. After a lot of work, I became the kind of person I wrote down on paper, and along the way, I acquired an apartment in a neighborhood where I always wanted to live, the neighborhood I drove around to give me inspiration to keep working when I slept on my mom's couch. As I looked around my apartment, I could almost not believe what I had accomplished and realized that all the work was worth it.

When I was twenty-nine, I met Jerry. He had an eight-year-old son he adored, and it was obvious how much family meant to him. He was such a kind man, and as we continued to date, I noticed the wonderful influence his parents had on him. He came from a very strong Italian family, and family was everything to them. We married two years after we met and had our first son, Dominic, two years later.

One example that made me realize the kind of incredible man I'd married happened a couple of months after Dominic's birth, and I was getting ready to return to running my fitness and marketing business. I went to Jerry crying and said, "I don't want to leave Dominic. I want to stay home."

His immediate response was, "Okay. I'll just work harder. My job is to do what's best for our family. If staying home is what is best for our family, then stay home."

I still sometimes look over at Jerry and cannot believe how lucky I am. However, I truly believe I would never have been ready for a healthy relationship if I hadn't put in all those years of work on myself, and if I hadn't done that work, I would have missed the best thing that has ever happened to me.

When I look back and think about my upbringing, I see my dad as a sad, hurt kid who didn't get to live a life. He had to start working when he was young, and his father introduced him to alcohol at a young age. The deck was stacked against him. He was never able to grow into the person he could have been.

My first son, Dominic, now has a younger brother, Antonio, who is four years younger than him, and an older step-brother, Zack, who is thirteen years older than him. I want them to know that a father is just as important as a mother, that there's a perfect yin and yang when a child has two parents in his or her life. It's a privilege and an honor as well as a responsibility to raise a family.

I'd tell a young person who is struggling with a parent who has an addiction that it's okay to be mad but to make allowances and consider what might have happened in their childhood that negatively impacted their parent's life. Appreciate them and look for their good qualities. Despite his flaws, my dad had some wonderful qualities, and I attribute a lot of my success in business to him.

But if you don't have someone to guide you, look around and find someone whose family life you aspire to and then work your ass off to break the cycle. It's always easier to repeat a pattern of behavior. It takes hard work and determination to break a pattern.

How Everclear's Art Alexakis Overcame Darkness

Before he gained fame as singer and guitarist in the rock band Everclear, Art Alexakis tried to kill himself. He got stoned, loaded sand in his pockets, and jumped off the Santa Monica Pier. After splashing into the water, his suicide attempt was thwarted when he heard his older brother, George, telling him to swim—his brother George who'd died of a heroin overdose.

George's death was not the only tragedy to befall Art. A year before his leap off the pier, Art's girlfriend had overdosed and died. Could Art's troubled childhood after his father abandoned him, his mother, his brother, and his three sisters have led him to take such a drastic act?

Absolutely.

In a study published in the *Journal of the American Academy of Child and Adolescent Psychiatry,* researchers Carmen Noemi Velez and Patricia Cohen state, "Living in a home without a dad is more highly correlated with suicide among children and teenagers than any other factor."

A Swedish study of more than a million children found that those in single-parent homes were more likely to commit suicide or attempt to do so than those with two parents. Boys had a higher risk of dying young from any cause and were also more likely than girls to develop psychiatric disease and narcotics related addiction disease. Another study of more than nine thousand students between the ages of fourteen and twenty revealed that broken homes (and the use of drugs and alcohol) were more common among those who attempted suicide. They were disproportionately female in this study and either lived with a single parent, in children's homes, or in foster homes.

Art's parents split up when he was six years old. He's had "splintered images" since the age of three of his dad's verbal and physical abuse of his mom. The separation and divorce was traumatic for the whole family. He has four older siblings, Paula, George, Kiki, and Vicky.

"It was a very brave thing for a woman to do in the sixties when there was still stigma about divorced women, but she did it because it was the right move for her children. Even though she's passed, I'm still very proud of her," Art said. He's a wonderful example of a man who turned his life around after a pain filled childhood and a history of drugs and alcohol addiction.

Art feels his dad should have simply moved down the street and helped raise him and his siblings. Instead, he moved to the other side of the country, married a younger woman, and raised her kids.

"I didn't really know him. He was still calling me Cowboy because the last time he knew me was when I was five or six and wanted to be a cowboy. My relationship with my dad was always like that. He called very sporadically, and literally like in the song, sent me five bucks on my birthday."

The song Art referenced? His hit single "Father of Mine," an autobiographical song on the 1998 Everclear album *So Much for the Afterglow* in which he sings about being a scared boy who lived in the projects and who was sometimes lucky enough to receive a birthday card and a five dollar bill from his dad.

Art never had the opportunity to build a relationship with his dad. He lived with him for a short while during his troubled teenage years, but they didn't connect. The death of rock icon David Bowie had a bigger impact on Art than the death of his father.

"It broke my heart because even though I'd only met him once in passing, as an artist, he'd given me so much over the years. And my dad didn't give me much. So that's my kind of juxtaposition—a rock star giving me more than my own father did."

The breakup of Art's parents was really hard on his older brother, George, whose overdose death happened when he was twenty-one and Art was twelve. At the time of the marital separation, Art's oldest sister, Paula, was already out of the house, a married mother at the age of seventeen or eighteen. After Paula came George, Kiki, and Vicky, who was five years older than Art. Art was the "accident baby" born in 1962 following the family's move from Detroit to California in the late 1950s.

The parental split destroyed them. The whole family was into drugs and alcohol, especially his brother and Paula's first husband. "It was rampant, and my sisters were kind of lost."

Art reflected on how kids and adults handled divorce at the time his parents split. "I think younger kids can adapt to divorce better, especially when the parents handle it better. But to be fair to both of them, very few people knew how to be divorced in the late 1960s. It was the last resort. There was a stigma. You were ashamed for life. It left a lot of damaged people like myself."

Art first tasted beer when he was three and tequila when he was six, and he loved alcohol. He progressed to dealing drugs when he was a bullied, skinny, twelve-year-old living in the projects. Between the ages of thirteen and twenty-two, he turned to hard drugs, indulging in a kaleidoscope of heroin, coke, acid, and speed, and suffered a near fatal overdose of his own. But it was alcohol that was his eventual downfall. "I was a blackout drunk. I'd gotten off hard drugs a few years earlier, and I put all the energy into drinking. And regardless of what people tell you, with the exception of maybe fentanyl, which is horrifying, nothing gets you more messed up than alcohol. Alcohol is just so vicious on your body, your soul, your spirit, and your mental capacity."

Art was in the habit of leaving work at lunchtime to get a drink, and sometimes he would not be seen for days. "My first wife, bless her heart, would go through bars looking for me because I'd just disappear. There were no cell phones or pagers back then. I'd show up two or three days later with my hands busted up and scrapes and bruises all over me. I wouldn't know how they got there, but I'd obviously been in fights."

What makes a person behave like that? Art's view is based on years of hard experience. "With addicts, it's like there's a hole inside of you and you're trying to fill that hole with anything that creates dopamine. It can be something as benign as sugar to something as vicious as heroin, cocaine, alcohol, sex. I would do things that were shameful, and it didn't bother me. I had incredibly low self-esteem."

Although he stresses he has to take some personal responsibility, the root cause of his ills was the family breakup and the violence, which had a horrible impact. Of course, not all of Art's memories are unhappy. There are happy memories too, like the time he displayed a child's enthusiasm for music. When Art was about three, his mom would leave the bedroom door ajar at night because he didn't like to sleep in the complete dark. One night when he heard music, he scampered into the living room to find Mom and Dad sitting on the couch drinking highballs.

The music that attracted his attention was that of The Beatles on the *Ed Sullivan Show*. "I couldn't control myself. I ran out in my jammies and started jumping around in front of the TV." His parents and siblings thought it was hilarious. It made a huge impression on him, and from that point on, he never wanted to do anything other than play music. At school, he didn't get great grades but was smart enough to do well on tests. His mom wanted him to go to college to study engineering or another subject that would lead to a solid career, but Art was more interested in creative endeavors like film classes.

When he met his second wife, Jenny, and she got pregnant, they moved back to Portland, Oregon, from San Francisco, not only because the schools were better in Portland, but also because there was a great music scene. The excitement of his daughter's birth in June 1992 gave way to postpartum depression. He says he felt like there was a great weight sitting on him.

He said to himself, I don't know what I'm doing. I can barely take care of myself, and now I have to take care of a child. "I was sitting there, and all of a sudden, I saw this light in the room, a beam, like a shot from God, and I realized I would always put her first and it would be okay. Even if I had to work three jobs and play in a band, I would put her first. That was my driving impetus, and it's never failed me."

Inspiration for the song "Father of Mine" came one night when he and Jenny were watching their daughter sleep. "You ever watch your kids sleep? Just watch 'em sleep? Other people think you're insane. It's a miracle. You made it together with your partner and it's a bonding experience. It's that sense of family that I never had growing up. It's cheap entertainment but man, it makes you feel really good."

That moment also made him reflect on his dad's behavior. "I thought, how does a guy walk away from this? How do you do that?" His wife went to bed, and he went to work. He picked up his acoustic guitar, played a couple of riffs, started writing words, and began building a story. "By the morning, I pretty much had all of it done." "Father of Mine" was created.

About two weeks later, he met with his Capital Records A&R (Artists and Repertoire) guy. Although he didn't usually do demos (something he says that, in hindsight, was really arrogant), he played the song for him. Art noticed the normally emotionless, stoic record company profession-al wiping his eyes behind his glasses. "I heard sobbing, and outside where the assistants had their desks were four young women hugging each other and weeping." The A&R guy later pushed for "Father of Mine" to be released as a single.

It became a hit and got Art attention everywhere he went. People from all backgrounds approached him and related their stories. Recently, a guy at a Starbucks told him, "You've changed my life."

His dad reached out to him. "Hey, boy, you wrote a song about me. I hope you did me proud," he said, in his strong Greek accent.

"Well, Dad, you haven't heard it," Art replied.

"No, I haven't heard it yet," his father admitted.

"Well," Art added, "it's honest and true."

"He didn't say much after that because I don't think he wanted to hear honest and true."

When one of Art's sisters was asked if he'd made a lot of it up, she said, "Arthur was being kind. If I'd written a song, it wouldn't have been that nice."

"They were older than me and saw a lot more of what was going on, like him smacking my mom or cheating on her with her best friends and neighbors," Art said. "My dad made a lot of bad choices. I have compassion for him because everybody makes bad choices and I've been the king of making bad choices, but I've never done so when it comes to my kids."

Art points to a destructive family history he managed to break. His Greek grandparents met when his grandmother was no more than thirteen or fourteen, and it was "kind of an arranged marriage" back in the old country. They came over on the boat after World War I in 1919, moved to New Hampshire, and had two children. When his grandmother became pregnant again, she ran off with a door-to-door salesman.

"Typical of men in my family, my grandfather took his sons, put them on a boat with a nanny, and sent them to be raised by his mom [in Greece] while he roamed the country-side having illegitimate children with other people. I come from a long line of men that adhered to that cycle, and I'm the first one that broke it because my mother raised me." So Art's father himself was an abandoned child who abandoned his own child. A typical cycle.

As Art's success grew, he was thrilled to be able to provide for his mom. Taking her to a platinum record party, he says, was "comedy gold. She was such a hillbilly from the Deep South, and when I told her she was going with me to the platinum party, she said, 'I don't know what the hell that is.'"

He flew her first class to LA, picked her up in a limo, and took her to the restaurant in Venice for an event that had all the Hollywood glitz and glamor: spotlights, red carpet, paparazzi.

"Boy, is this for you?" she asked.

"Yes, Mama."

"What is this platinum thing?"

"It means I sold a million records."

"A million people bought your noisy rock and roll record?"

"Yeah. Imagine that. And it's probably going double platinum."

"That's two million? And this is for you?"

"Yes, Mama."

Then she got into the mood of the occasion, stepped out of the limo, and waved to the crowd. Her attitude: I always knew he was going to be something special.

Art is thankful that his success enabled him to buy a house for his mom and pay for her care while his oldest sister took care of her physically until she died of cancer in 2016. Art is glad his mom got to meet his wife Vanessa and that he was able to spend more time with his mom toward the end.

His childhood experience has greatly influenced the way Art sees himself as a parent. "As a father, I take it so seriously, this honor of being a parent, because everything, negative or positive, affects your children somewhere down the line, especially being a male role model for my daughters. Our family is so strong right now, and that's because of my sobriety. I'm about to hit thirty-four years sober. I work my program really hard. I have a great fellowship. I just love what I do."

Art says his goals in life were to play guitar in a rock and roll band, have a family, and own a house with a white picket fence. "That's basically what I've got, except I have a nice wall with electric paint instead of the white picket fence," he jokes.

"I went from being a kid that grew up in a housing project that had always struggled for money to making millions, and it was a different world. Getting that big house up on the hill . . . it's much better looking out than looking in. I'm even grateful for the hard things because they make me a better person, learning from them and pushing through them. With my father not being there, it taught me to fend for myself in a lot of ways that I shouldn't have at such a young age, but I'm grateful for the strength it gave me. Now with my children, I want them to find their bliss but also be able to monetize it to make a living."

He says the relationships with his wife and people he's known for years are better because of his sobriety and his relationship with a higher power. After being diagnosed with multiple sclerosis in 2016, he came out with "Hot Water Test" in 2019, a song about it. More recently, he was told he has pancreatitis. "Getting old sucks, but I'm a sixty-one-year-old guy with MS and I get to play rock and roll for a living. I mean, come on. That's a good gig, you think? I will be a ninety-year-old guy with bad hearing just pissing everybody off at the old folks' home, just cranking it up. Hopefully, they'll have a punk rock old folks' home."

Meanwhile, he's grateful for the impact that "Father of Mine" has had on people from all kinds of backgrounds because "parental abandonment is not something that's relegated to just one section of our society. It's pervasive."

And before he gets to the old folks' home, his priority is to be the father that his father never was.

"One of the things about the high divorce rate is that we've learned to be better at raising children in divorce. My wife has a stepdaughter. Sometimes you get along with your stepchild's mother or father; sometimes you don't. You gotta grind it out and be there and be positive and find love. Put your kids first and raise 'em up."

Chapter 4

Chef Al's Recipe for Recovery

Substance abuse is rampant in America today. Especially among youth. And especially for adolescents who don't have the benefit of a father in the home.

According to the National Center for Fathering, children without fathers are ten times more likely to abuse chemical substances and 71 percent of all children who abuse substances come from fatherless homes. Other research has found that 75 percent of adolescent patients in chemical abuse centers come from homes without a father.

Studies suggest that children of parents with an alcohol abuse disorder could well develop the same issues (or abuse other substances), drink at an early age, engage in risky behavior, and have to navigate mental health issues. One study found they are also likely to have interpersonal problems, school performance issues, and difficulties with their own parenting later in life. That's not all. They are also more likely to become victims of sexual abuse, have a greater frequency of run-ins with the law, are more likely to have suicidal tendencies, and even have an increased chance of being admitted to the emergency room for accidents.

Anecdotally, many individuals tell vivid stories of life-threatening addictions they have overcome. No one would imagine, for instance, the difficult road that celebrity chef Ashish Alfred has traveled on his way to success.

Owner of three acclaimed restaurants in the Washington-Baltimore metropolitan area, Chef Al, as he's often called, honestly admits, "I almost died twice." Chef Al grew up in Montgomery County, Maryland, and his mother was a driven, hard worker en route to business success. When Ashish was young, his dad was around a lot, but as Ashish got older and his dad struggled with alcoholism, his father's presence in the house dwindled. Ashish says his older brother, George, ten years his senior "was as much a parent to me as anyone else."

In third or fourth grade, Ashish began having discipline issues and problems with his academic performance. At that time, he began to notice the problems at home. "When I was younger, I was oblivious to the tension, the stress, and at times, the violence."

His dad's alcoholism often took a nasty turn. "I remember him popping up sometimes late at night, and there would be some sort of crescendo that ended with the police arriving or him just leaving." Once Ashish called 911 because his father was throwing things at his mother and abusing her. "I didn't see him for long periods of time. I remember being dropped off to see him at an apartment where he was staying for a while."

Naturally, a young son misses his dad's presence no matter what. "From what my mother told me, at a young age I longed for him very desperately. As much as in many ways I was afraid of him, I longed for the love that I knew he was capable of giving me. It was very painful for me."

When Ashish was nine, George left for college in California. That made Ashish "the only man in my mother's life, for better or worse. We were all each other had for a very long time. It was tough having a front row seat to the stress and emotion of my mother trying to build a business, doing it alone, trying to raise a young man, and dealing with my father, who was at the height of his addiction."

The family dynamic had other effects. "I was a pretty lonely kid. I struggled for a while to fit in. I eventually became the kind of young man that would do anything to get friends." That included ignoring schoolwork, getting into violent altercations, drinking to excess, and generally "acting like a moron."

In a profile of Chef Al, the *Washington Post* revealed that he was suspended from school after hacking into a teacher's computer to change a grade and was kicked out the following year. At a new school, "I made friends with some real criminals. That's when it clicked that the more I drank, the more drugs I did, the more fights I got in, the more popular I was."

By the time he was in eighth grade, he was buying pot, stealing booze, and drinking a good part of the day. His father was in and out of his life, and when his parents were separated during his drinking binges, his mom sent Ashish to his father's apartment to make sure he hadn't accidentally burned the place down when he was drinking and smoking cigarettes. "I stopped being a kid while I was still a kid," he admitted.

Ashish loved hospitality. His mom opened her first assisted living home in 1991 and his father had a background in hotels. "Whether they meant to teach me or not, they took great pride in caring for others. I don't know if that stuck with me because I knew it was the one way I could really impress my dad." At sixteen, Ashish worked as a host and progressed to being a barback.

Watching the effect alcohol had on his father initially gave Ashish respect for alcohol, but by the time he was seventeen or eighteen, he started drinking heavily. "Binge drinking was a big deal. Shot gunning beers. Alcohol was a way not just to numb myself but also to feel like king of the world. I could have a conversation with anybody, belong in any group. Alcohol bought me entrance, was my cover charge."

Ashish began experimenting with drugs in his early twenties. Working at a gentlemen's club, he obtained drugs for guests. His drinking and cocaine habits spiraled out of control and his mother kicked him out. A girlfriend did the same. And then so did the friends who'd let him couch surf.

"I burned every bridge, owed everyone money, and went home with my tail between my legs," he said.

Ashish caught the cooking bug watching the Food Network on TV and persuaded his mother to pay for tuition and rent so he could attend the French Culinary Institute in New York. Although his mother signed the paperwork for him to attend culinary school, her fear of his unreliability made her question how much it would cost her if he quit after two weeks. She asked a similar question when helping him rent an apartment. What was the liability if he broke the lease in a month?

The culinary school turned out to be the perfect place for Ashish. "I enjoyed the structure and being told what to do because the heat, the pressure, the violence of the kitchen was nothing new to me." He'd watched his mother build a business and his brother made sure he did his chores. "It was nothing new to have somebody breathing down my neck, screaming at me." And with his father, "If you didn't move fast enough, he moved you." Culinary school, he says, was a cakewalk, "although I didn't think I was going to be the next Iron Chef."

After he graduated from culinary school, Ashish stayed in New York, working at restaurants. "I held jobs for as long as I could, and I'd inevitably get banged up, miss work for a couple of days, and get fired. It's a very common pattern in the hospitality industry. Somebody will work somewhere for a little while until their demons really show up and then find another job and do the same thing. It came to a point where I had burned enough bridges, and I was physically unhealthy."

He was a party animal, sold coke, and got arrested twice for DUI, so his mom insisted he return to the DC area. She financially backed a restaurant for him, and both of them thought it would straighten him out. But it did the opposite. "What did I know about opening a restaurant, training a staff, or running a P&L? I knew nothing. I had a little bit of my mother's money, a handful of beer, and a pocket full of coke. It opened super undercapitalized with no real plan in place, and inevitably, it failed. It wouldn't work because I wasn't working the way I was supposed to work."

Ashish didn't show up for work. Heroin and booze were in control. The rock-bottom moment that got him on the path to sobriety came after a night of shooting up heroin with a prostitute. Out of cash, he went to his restaurant, 4935 Kitchen Bar, where he yanked open the locked panic bar door after realizing he didn't have his keys and removed cash from the safe. Back at the apartment, he passed out. When he woke up, the prostitute and the cash were gone. A week later, his mom drove him four hours to be admitted into a twenty-eight-day rehabilitation program in Pennsylvania.

"Eventually my mother got wise and realized I wasn't going to fix myself and there had to be some sort of catalyst," he said. "She told me, 'I love you very much and I'm very sorry for what you've been through in your life and how your life has transpired, but none of that is my fault. At some point, you have to take ownership of it. I have to push you aside until you decide to do something for yourself.'"

Ashish returned to rehab which—this time—worked. "I'd already been to jail. I'd tried rehab a couple times before." It was either get help or die. "I came home in a clear head space and better equipped."

He opened Duck, Duck, Goose, a French bistro, based on his experiences working in small brasserie-style restaurants in New York, and he says he made some promises to God, himself, and his family.

Now that he's sober, is it difficult to work in the restaurant industry which, according to the Department of Health and Human Services, has the highest rate of substance abuse among all industries? Although he admits he's had some slips along the way, he's not inclined to go for drinks after work because everyone else is. He admits that having patience with people who are actively addicted can be difficult because he knows there is help out there. His advice to troubled young people? "If you think you have a problem, you probably have a problem. There's help if you want it."

Ashish got the help he needed, and his stellar career is a testament to what a person in recovery can do. "The restaurants have helped me build a platform for myself. They have become a pedestal for me to do something on my own." To that end, he is working on book and TV opportunities.

There's no doubt he owes a lot to his ever-present mother. "I have an amazing, beautiful relationship with my mother. I know I can count on her, and she's very certain she can count on me."

The relationship with his dad is more complex. In spite of his alcoholism, his father was always a cheerleader for him, and he's thankful for that. His father got sober several years ago, but Ashish doesn't see him much since he lives overseas. Still, he adds, "I think my father's sobriety gave me the gift of sobriety."

That's a good legacy.

Chapter 5

From Abuse to Hope

The night he was conceived, Victor Marx's dad put a pistol to his mom's head and shoved rosary beads down her throat. It was a portent of things to come. One of his earliest memories is being tied to a bed and abused. Between the ages of three and seven, he was repeatedly and horribly mistreated. He was even dumped in a tub until he passed out and once was deliberately and painfully shocked.

"The professionals call it torture," Victor says. "I thank God that he kept me alive to be able to tell my story in a way that's redemptive but gives other people hope, including children, both here in the US and around the world."

The US Department of Health and Human Services says more than fifteen million children live in homes in which domestic violence has happened at least once and they're at greater risk for repeating the cycle as adults by entering into abusive relationships or becoming abusers themselves. A boy who sees his mother being abused is ten times more likely to abuse his female partner as an adult, while a girl who grows up in a home where her father abuses her mother is more than six times as likely to be sexually abused as a girl who didn't see such abuse.

Children who witness or are victims of emotional, physical, or sexual abuse are, as adults, at higher risk for mental and physical health problems such as depression, anxiety, poor self-esteem, diabetes, obesity, and heart disease.

According to the Centers for Disease Control and Prevention (CDC), at least one in seven children have experienced child abuse or neglect in the past year, a number that's probably an underestimate because many cases are unreported. In 2020, 1,750 children died of abuse and neglect in the United States, and rates of child abuse and neglect are five times higher for children in poor families.

Apart from the immediate effects, including physical injuries such as cuts, bruises, or broken bones, chronic abuse may result in toxic stress, which can change brain development and increase the risk for problems like post-traumatic stress disorder (PTSD) and learning, attention, and memory difficulties. But there's always hope, and Victor is a classic example of someone who has overcome adversity.

He has told his story candidly and passionately in a podcast interview with me, in a YouTube video, on his website, and speaking to all kinds of audiences. From such a traumatic childhood, he has built a life as a powerful humanitarian in which his faith keeps him strong while helping women and children in dire situations in the US and abroad. It's a remarkable journey for someone born into terrible circumstances.

"My mother could have aborted me, but she didn't," he said. "And I always try to be more grateful for the things that didn't happen than the things that did. I think it's a trap when people who come from challenged backgrounds stay stuck in being a victim by saying I survived this. You've got to move from surviving to thriving. The journey is not necessarily pretty."

There is no avoiding the fact that Victor's early years were not pretty, and he certainly endured horrors no child should experience. His biological dad left before he was born. His mom married six times, and as a vulnerable kid, the youngest of four, he attended fourteen schools and lived in seventeen homes. "Moving was a normal thing for us."

His mother met a highly intelligent former military intelligence officer who turned out to be a pedophile. "He had challenges in his life of perversion and addiction. I was one of the siblings that suffered under that. He tortured me and abused me from the ages of three to seven." Frequently molested, Victor was even left in a commercial cooler to die after being abused by a neighborhood kid. Later in life, he visited a trauma specialist more than one hundred and twenty times "to try to get my head together," and he believes many of his challenges came from severe post-traumatic stress.

Victor's tormentor also abused his mom. "He held a pistol at her head numerous times. He would make her confess to things she never did. He would threaten to kill us kids. Do I think she knew some of the things that were going on? Yeah. Was she able to compartmentalize? Yeah. Other things, she had no clue. She was a very broken person."

His mom, he says, was diagnosed with dissociative identity disorder, which is a mental health disorder in which someone has two or more personalities. "Under high stress, she would just check out. We've talked about it a lot as adults, and in tears, she says she didn't know what was going on, which isn't uncommon. People who abuse children are very good at hiding it."

Around the age of ten, Victor experienced the power of Jesus Christ for the first time when his stepdad arrived home drunk one night waving a gun and shooting lights outside the house. Victor, his mother, and his siblings cowered in the closet while his stepdad shouted, "Come out, I'm coming in."

His mother prayed, "The blood of Jesus covers the door. The blood of Jesus covers the door."

"Jesus is a nice guy," Victor said to his mother. "He's kind and compassionate. He's not going to stop that evil man. We need somebody strong. We need a Rambo Jesus." Somehow, his stepfather was held back from entering and passed out in his bedroom. "The prayer worked. We escaped that night through a window."

Not surprisingly, considering his home life, Victor got into trouble at school, even in the first grade. Once he stuck his finger into the classroom hamster cage until he got bitten and bloodied. Another time, he hopped on the back of a utility truck and rode it all the way out of the playground. As the years went by, he was sent out of class to the school office multiple times with teachers asking, "What is wrong with you, boy?"

He'd find a teacher he preferred and go sit in her class. "When you're a child, you can't really process extreme abuse. Innately, there was something wrong with me because I kept getting in trouble."

In middle school, Victor hung out with the cool kids who were smart and athletic and liked by all the girls. "They let me hang out with them, I guess because I was part crazy. I'd throw water balloons at passing cars. I'd do about anything to get accepted."

Victor fondly remembers going to the home of a friend, John McClendon, and how kind the family was to him. "I thought it was the coolest thing that they had waffles and certain cereals for breakfast I'd never seen because we were so poor. My mom was struggling with six kids and no support from the fathers. The McClendon home was such a place of hope that it would get me along to the next crisis in my life. I remember thinking, one day I want to have a family like the McClendons." In his forties, Victor reconnected with them to express his appreciation, although by that time, the father had died.

After Victor and his family (without a stepfather) moved into an apartment complex, his older brother became friends with a neighborhood girl whose father frequently traveled. One night the police knocked on their door and told them, "We need you to come with us." The girl had killed herself with a shotgun. The cops showed them the ugly aftermath and asked, "Do you know anything about this?" To this day, Victor doesn't know why the cops wanted to expose them to the gory suicide scene.

During high school, Victor participated in sports and music and played in the school band. Girls told him he was cute, and he told them he didn't want to be cute. By this time, his mom was on her fourth or fifth marriage, this time to a guy who was a well paid commercial diver. When Victor was suspended during his sophomore year, his mom told his step-dad, "You need to discipline Victor. You need to whoop him."

His stepdad carved a two-by-four into a paddle and struck him a few times until Victor retaliated. "I turned around and said, 'Don't. I'm a full-gown man. I'm not going to be hit or hurt by anyone else.' He saw my eyes were kind of crazy, the kind of look that says I'll wait for you to go to sleep and get even."

His stepdad wasn't fazed. "If you ever get in my face again or threaten me I'll take you out back," he said, meaning he would use the paddle again, or worse.

"Fine," said Victor. "I don't care."

"But I want you to see something first," his stepfather replied.

He walked Victor into the house, pulled a briefcase from underneath his bed, took out some newspaper clippings, and said, "Read this before you ever get in my face again." There was a photo of a guy in handcuffs standing in front of a judge. The story reported he'd shot a couple of guys in a barfight, killing one, and was sent to Chino prison in California. It was Victor's stepfather.

Victor called his mom, who was at work. "Hey, mom, do you know you married a murderer?"

"Of course I do."

"Well, when were you going to tell us? Isn't this something we should know?"

"I figured I'd tell you sometime or you'd find out when you needed to know. Apparently, you needed to know today."

Victor went back to his stepfather. "Hey, what's up, step-pops? We're good, right?"

He didn't want to mess with a murderer. "He did the best he could. He married a woman with four kids that grew to a family of six kids. He was actually a good stepfather," Victor said.

His stepdad later told him he'd been in a biker gang and shot the two guys after they threatened him. Thinking they were both dead and not wanting to go to prison, he shot himself but survived. While unconscious, he had a near-death experience in which he went to heaven and the Lord told him, "You can't come yet. You have a mission." The mission was to marry a woman with six children!

Victor says he barely graduated high school and worked in a department store during the day. At night, he worked as a bouncer at a bar, "a little kid trying to be a bouncer."

Then on October 23, 1983, a suicide bomber drove a truck bomb into the US Marines barracks in Beirut, Lebanon, killing 241 American military personnel and wounding 128. It was the biggest loss of Marines in a single day since the Battle of Iwo Jima in World War II. Victor saw it on TV, and it had a huge impact on him.

"It was what I needed to direct all this anger in me." He went to the Marines recruiting office and signed for a three-year stint, a life-altering decision. "The Marine Corps taught me discipline and gave me skill sets I never had and showed me how powerful the human mind is. I learned my mind is far more powerful than my body."

Six months before the end of his time with the Marines, Victor received a letter that further changed his life. It was from his biological dad, someone with whom he'd never had a connection and had seen only once at the age of six. He thought of his stepdad as his real dad. The letter began "Dear son," and that made him mad. "I thought, Don't call me son.

All you did was get my mom pregnant. You've never been a dad to me. I was so offended."

"I know you think I'm crazy," his father wrote.

Victor did think he was crazy. He'd been in a mental hospital for homicidal tendencies, and it was the same mental hospital his own father had died in.

"I am crazy. But this time for Jesus Christ," his father added in the letter. He said he'd surrendered his life to Jesus. His dad went on to apologize for not being a dad and asked if Victor would visit him in Louisiana. The letter was so compelling, Victor took leave from the Marines and did so.

He found a man who'd been a fighter, like his father before him, with a flat, broken nose to show for it and big tattooed forearms. Still, Victor saw something within him, some niceness.

His dad invited him to church along with some fighters he was training, including black belts. It was June 22, 1986, a transformational day in Victor's life.

"All of a sudden I could feel the love of God, and that was the beginning of my walk with him. I'd let my heart turn hard, and I realized I'd done wrong. Nothing as heinous as torture and abuse of children, but if you look at the Ten Commandments, I about broke them all. I was ready to be forgiven and to surrender my life for a greater purpose than anything I could ever think of."

Victor's reconciliation with his dad was not all plain sailing. "It was rough. You don't get a pass for never being there."

They exchanged words on a drive one day. "Boy, you're like me," his dad said, pulling over on a fast two-lane highway. They got out, stood in front of the car, and squared up to each other. "Come on. Let's do it. Come get all you want," his dad said, challenging him. Victor's father was an eighth degree black belt in judo and a jujitsu boxer. It would not be a fair fight.

"He made fists that looked like clubs," Victor said. "I thought, man these cars are whizzing by. If we start fighting, one of us or both of us is going to get run over." So Victor suggested they fight later and his father agreed to that. They never did. "I have sparred with him and been hit by him, and it was like getting hit by a doggone telephone pole."

Victor's faith led him to become a devout churchgoer. It also eventually led him to his wife, Eileen. When he saw her walk into church for the first time, he was stunned. He found her breathtakingly beautiful. A winner of the Miss Fitness USA competition, she had a career as a fitness instructor. She also gave her life to Christ, they became friends, and she invited him to dinner at the Vera Cruz Fish House in San Marcos, California to celebrate his twenty-second birthday.

"Her green eyes drew me in. I went home that night and wrote about it in my little prayer journal." Victor says he'd previously prayed, "Lord, whoever my future wife is, please protect her right now."

That night, he says, the Lord told him, "This is the woman you've been praying for." Victor was ready to marry her, but the Lord told him to slow down.

And there was one big obstacle: Eileen already had a boyfriend. One day she entered the church to seek counseling from the pastor. She was having problems with the boyfriend because he wanted to party all the time. She said to Victor, "I'm a new Christian. I don't want to do that. What do you think?"

Victor thought it was his golden opportunity and didn't mince his words. "I'll tell you what I think. I think that dude is like the spawn of Satan, and you should drop him like a bad habit. Now that we've got that settled, I'm looking for a wife, and I don't even date. I just want to get married and probably be a missionary in Africa living just above the poverty line."

Victor said Eileen responded more maturely. "That's very sweet of you to offer. Let me pray."

It didn't take long. At 5:30 the next morning she called, crying. "Victor, I know you have emotions for me. But I've got to make sure this guy I'm dating isn't the one for me."

A year later, they were still friends. He owned karate studios, and she was working at one of them. He went to her house for a small dinner party. Things had changed. A spark ignited. He proposed three months later, and they married three months after that. "We made an intentional decision not to have sex until after we were married. I cherished her so much, it took me a month and a half to even ask to hold her hand."

Thirty-five years later, they're still married and have five children and five grandchildren. They decided to have a baby as soon as they were married. When she broke the news that she was expecting, Victor said he excitedly hugged and kissed her. And then he got terrified. His fear was that he didn't know how to be a dad. He hadn't had a good example in his life. Eileen held his hand and reassured him. Then God's spirit told him, "I'll teach you everything." Victor was comforted, knowing that the Bible says God is our father.

The couple had three children back-to-back, took a ten-year break, and then had two more. How did he feel when his children were at the age when he was abused? "It triggered me," he admitted. "I looked at them and thought, who in hell would abuse a kid? Who would torture a child?"

When his kids were older, Victor asked them what he could have done differently. "They said I was a great dad but overprotective. I was hypervigilant, which was part of the PTSD. It was miserable. People think it's just worry, but it was extreme anxiety where I was waking up three times a night, checking the doors and windows."

Life as an adult, husband, and father has not been without its challenges. He and his wife separated twice but never wanted to divorce, both having come from divorced families. "In thirty-five years, I've never cheated on my wife or been cheated on." His advice: "If you're single, I say, start purity now. If you're married, make sure your marriage is pure."

Reflecting on his faith journey, Victor says he was born Catholic, raised Baptist, and went through charismatic Pentecostal experiences. "I knew about Jesus, always believed in God, but I couldn't really relate to him at that age because people referred to him as God the Father and all the fathers I knew were absent, angry, drunkards, violent, or abusive. But his son, Jesus, was different, since I heard all the Sunday school stories, and he loved the little children."

Today, Victor runs a nonprofit organization, All Things Possible Ministries, which conducts humanitarian missions as far afield as Iraq, Syria, North Africa, and Southeast Asia, often in high threat environments, helping orphans and widows. He says that the discipline of military life and faith in God helped him recover from his traumatic childhood and gives him the strength to help others.

He focuses his attention on hunting predators and rescuing women and children held captive by traffickers and other abusers. In the process, he has helped over forty-five thousand children. When ISIS invaded Iraq, killing, and beheading people, and taking young women and even kids for sex trafficking, All Things Possible Ministries took a team to help out. More recently, within seventy-two hours of the brutal Hamas attack on Israel, Victor and his team accepted an invitation to go to the beleaguered country and visit with families most affected while rockets rained down.

The US doesn't have those kinds of dangers, but our culture, he says, is significantly undermined in other ways. "The greatest threat to America is simply the lack of men to be fathers."

Victor's advice to young men going through tough times who should become the caring fathers of the future? "First, it's a cliché, but tough times don't last. Second, don't just kick away from tough times. And in a weird way, embrace it. In the Marines we called it embrace the suck. It will help build character. Third, if you have abuse in your background, the shame is not yours. It was never yours, so don't make someone else's perversion into your shame. It's on them. And finally, keep hope, faith, and love in front of you. And the best person who has ever embodied that is the God man, Jesus Christ of Nazareth."

Chapter 6

Beyond Sex Trafficking

In the hit movie *Taken,* Liam Neeson stars as a heroic father who almost single-handedly rescues his beautiful teenage daughter after she's kidnapped in Paris to be sold as a sex slave. It's a dramatic action-packed thriller that spawned two sequels. But that is the world of moviemaking and not the real world.

"Unfortunately, it had the unintended effect of completely miseducating the public about what human trafficking is, how it happens, and who it happens to," says Catherine Chen, chief executive officer of Polaris, a national nonprofit organization that runs the US National Human Trafficking Hotline.

The reality is that most victims are not kidnapped. More often than not, they know their traffickers and maybe even trust or love them. Often they don't see themselves as victims. The Polaris group puts it this way: "They have been so expertly manipulated or 'groomed' that they believe they are making their own choice to engage in commercial sex. These emotional ties are as powerful as being held in handcuffs or behind bars."

They add, "Traffickers target vulnerable people who have needs that the traffickers can fill. Sometimes they offer material support—a place to live, a chance to get rich quick. Other times they offer love, emotional support, or a sense of belonging. Kidnapping victims and forcing them into the sex trade through violence is rare."

Sadly, most cases of human trafficking are never reported. But since its inception in 2007, the National Human Trafficking Hotline has received more than four hundred thousand reports and identified more than one hundred and fifty thousand victims.

As mentioned earlier, the Institute for Shelter Care reports that 70 percent of exploited women grew up without a father in the home, adding, "We believe that dads make a difference, and their involvement in the lives of their daughters can stem the epidemic of sexual exploitation. When dads are absent or uninvolved in the lives of their children, those children are significantly more likely to face challenges." The institute's executive director, Jeanne Allert, PhD, says, "The greatest insulation a girl has against being exploited is a healthy relationship with her father."

Traffickers prey upon children whose basic needs are unmet. Yvonne Williams, executive director of the Trafficking in America Task Force, says that a host of social problems feed the pipeline of child trafficking. In addition to fatherless homes, there is poverty, teen runaways, an increase in kids posting their images on the internet, and the pernicious rise in child pornography.

The Institute for Shelter Care study "Domestic Minor Familial Sex Trafficking" states, "The modern-day trafficker has too often been characterized as a cunning and patient outsider, an all-in-the-shadows manipulator, able to exert his or her control through promises, money, drugs, or romance. Now, twenty years into the anti-trafficking movement within the United States, another reality is to be confronted: that sometimes the perpetrator is not an outsider, but rather, an intimate threat residing within the home and heart of the victim."

Of growing concern is the prevalence of social media in the lives of today's youth. According to Empower Her Network, an organization that helps survivors of human trafficking, between 2000 and 2021, 55 percent of sex trafficking victims in the US were recruited online using social media, messaging platforms, and dating apps. Trafficking skyrocketed in 2020. On Facebook, recruitment increased 125 percent over the previous year and on Instagram by 95 percent.

Just about anyone can fall victim. Rachel Thomas, a member of Empower Her Network's board of directors, and CEO of Ending the Game, an intervention curriculum for victims of commercial sexual exploitation, was a high-performing college student when she was trafficked after accepting an invitation to be in a music video.

"If you have a kid at home longing to fit in, or go on a first date, or get on television, sex trafficking might suddenly feel like it hits a little closer to home," according to advice on the Empower Her Network website. "Really pay attention to what they have access to, how they're using what they have access to, and who they're connecting with."

Children are eleven times more likely to suffer sexual and physical abuse in single-family homes, especially when it's the father who is absent. Without parental protection, kids are more likely to run away from home, go missing, or end up in the foster care system. That in itself is a monumental concern since the National Center for Missing and Exploited Children found that in 2016, 86 percent of sex trafficking victims were in the care of social services when they went missing.

Shared Hope International, a nonprofit leader in the fight to eradicate domestic minor sex trafficking, said in its "National Report on Domestic Minor Sex Trafficking" that 70 percent of victims endured physical or sexual abuse before being trafficked, and the risk of being trafficked increased exponentially for runaways. Shockingly, according to an article on its website, one in three girls are trafficked within forty-eight hours of running away. "A girl's most vulnerable point is simply her age. Young girls are often more susceptible to rely on the perceived love and support that a pimp initially offers." And the average age someone first trades sex is just under sixteen, according to research by Center for Court Innovation.

Two victims of sex trafficking spoke openly and bravely to me about their harrowing experiences and how they have turned from victims to victors helping others who find themselves in the same predicament.

Annette's Story

Annette's parents divorced when she was young, and she didn't get to see much of her father. She was left living with her mother, brother, and sister in low-income housing. In the summer months, while her siblings went out of town to visit her mom's family, she stayed at her paternal grandmother's house.

Mostly, her father was gone, and she never got any attention from her mother. Her mother even seemed to avoid her friends and was not involved in school activities. "My friends at school never saw her. I think it was because I looked more like my father, while my brother looked more like her. It affected me because she was so beautiful, and I wanted people to see how she was."

When she was twelve or thirteen, Annette was sent to an institution. "It was an institution for bad kids or kids who have nowhere to go," she said, stating what she thought the purpose of the place was at the time. "Something bad happened in the family and the police came and got me and my brother. I thought I was a bad child. I just did everything wrong as far as my mother was concerned, and she didn't want me no more. She gave me to the system."

Annette was at the institution for almost two years and loved it, even though the woman who ran the house was a Catholic nun who "used to whoop me with switches." Family members didn't visit. "It was a different atmosphere from growing up in the projects," Annette said. "I got to meet new people, and it seemed like everyone was like me."

Back home in Cleveland, her mom sent Annette to live with her aunt when Annette was fifteen, and she was bussed to school on the east side. "I got chased to the bus stop and beat up all the time." For a while, she got to do whatever she wanted to do, and nobody made sure she was in school. She joined a gang. For a year and a half, the gang was like a family to her. Then the guys she hung out with robbed someone who died, and they were imprisoned. "My world was turned upside down when that happened."

Annette went to a new school, met a new guy, and became pregnant at sixteen. For a while, the two teenage parents continued to attend school and helped raise their baby son by doing part-time jobs. Eventually, when they broke up, her boyfriend's mother took the baby into her home.

Annette got a job working for the housing authority because they wanted someone who lived in the projects, but her life inevitably revolved around alcohol and drugs. "I began drinking and smoking weed. My family were functional addicts. If you didn't smoke and drink with the family, you just didn't belong with the family."

Then, despite holding a steady job for ten years, she began to experiment with harder drugs. "Nobody, absolutely nobody, ever asked me if there was anything wrong with me."

When she got into a car accident, Annette walked away from her government job because she knew she would fail a drugs test. She also walked away from a live-in relationship with a man who had a good career and was financially supportive because she discovered he was cheating on her. Annette moved into a house where the rent was really low, but she had no income and desperately needed money for drugs.

"I decided I was going to go out and sell my body. I was gonna go out and prostitute," she said, bluntly. In the beginning, she thought it was fine, but the life took an ugly turn. "It got bad. I ran into people who beat me, raped me, and wouldn't pay me."

Annette became homeless. All her worldly possessions were held in one bag. She slept anywhere she could lay her head for the night: abandoned houses, under bridges, at bus stops, in the bushes. "I ended up living with other druggie guys that would steal drugs."

One day a young woman seemingly came to her rescue. She told Annette she could see how much she was suffering in the freezing cold and had a place where Annette could stay. She'd even get her a little something—drugs—to hold her over. She got into that house and couldn't get out. "I was out of the cold, but the people who gave me the drugs wouldn't let me leave. That was the first time I was trapped."

They sold her for sex.

"They kept selling me and selling me saying I owed them for the drugs they kept giving me. They would give me the drugs, and I had to do things with the men."

The worst was to come. The dope dealers trafficked Annette to another dealer who installed her in a hotel room where she was forced into sex with a seemingly never-ending stream of men. She went to prison several times for possession and solicitation. She had to get high, and the only way she thought she could pay for the drugs was to sell her body. The cycle repeated for fifteen to twenty years.

Annette's luck changed when she found herself in the Human Trafficking Specialized Docket at Cleveland Municipal Court run by Judge Marilyn Cassidy. Annette says she didn't even know what human trafficking was, but she was a victim. "The judge was amazing," she says. "She was asking people, 'How can I help you?'" Annette agreed to go to the Renee Jones Empowerment Center, a nonprofit organization that helps human trafficking victims get their lives back together.

Her first surprise came when she arrived at their office the next day. "A young lady greeted me, shook my hand, and treated me like a human." Then she met Renee Jones. "She didn't ask me if I was a drug addict or had been to jail. She didn't say this is what we're going to do. She asked me, 'How can I help you? What do you need?'" Annette joined a two-year course and graduated in eighteen months.

The human trafficking docket and the Renee Jones Empowerment Center helped Annette rebuild her life, and as a result, she pays it forward, speaking on the center's behalf, offering other survivors hope for a better life. "I feel honored to be able to do it. I didn't have a voice and now I do."

Her advice: "You cannot do anything without knowing yourself first. Remember the tough times because that's going to help you with your future. It won't be easy, but if you know yourself, it can get you along the way."

The other major step she has taken is to reunite with family members. "It was hard because I had to let them know the truth. I have nothing but blessings from them." She is totally connected with her son. "He thinks I can save the world."

After so many years, even though she never really knew her father, at least she has a family again, and through sharing her story and helping others, her life has meaning.

Camille's Story

Growing up in Nashville, Tennessee, Camille lived in what she describes as a normal middle class family. It changed when, at the age of nine, she discovered her father was really her stepfather—and a monster.

"He molested me and my oldest sister, and it went on for years," she said.

Camille found out he was her stepdad by accident when she overheard a conversation with her mom in which he mentioned he was not her biological father. Camille told me that the abuse began when she was only five years old. "Back then you didn't tell. You did what your mother and father said. If not, you'd get beat or a whooping. I never said anything about it." But the result was that she acted out in school.

Her stepfather's abuse was not exposed until she was about eleven and after they moved to a bigger home. She found photos of her sister hidden under her parents' mattress and showed them to her mom. As soon as her truck driver stepdad went out of town, her mom went to the authorities.

"When he came back, the police was waiting for him. It was on the news and in the newspaper that he had molested two of his children." That changed the lives of her and her older sister who was pregnant by the stepdad.

How did she feel when he was arrested?

"I had no emotions. You're young and being abused in that type of way, being molested, you kind of suppress your feelings. You don't really know how to address some of the things you feel about the whole situation."

Encouraged by her mom, Camille had her first job at thirteen and graduated high school at sixteen. But she'd already turned to sex and drugs.

"By the age of thirteen, I was sexually active. By the age of sixteen, I was using drugs. I attracted older guys, maybe five to twenty years older than I was. I gravitated toward them. For the older men, it was like a trophy to have a younger woman."

What Camille got out of it was whatever she could get from the men with whom she was sexually active. It seemed glamorous and made her feel like an adult. "Being that I was into the drug scene and with older people, I thought I had it going on, and I thought I was grown."

When she was nineteen, Camille was abducted by a stranger, taken to another state, and put into a life of sexual exploitation and prostitution. Thanks to the drug addiction, she was easy prey. She ran into three guys one day. "I'd never seen them a day in my life, but they had drugs."

In many ways, she says, she was still a child. "Now that I'm older, I like to say it was a robbery in process. I was robbed of my life, of what could have been."

One abductor took her from state to state. "I was mentally, physically, spiritually broken down." She says she was in that abusive relationship from about 1989 to 1996, dragged across thirty-two states, and had children with him.

"After a while, when the kids started coming along, I was the recruiter and brought other women in." Camille was trapped to such an extent that she'd tell him, "You don't need anybody else. I can do this for you." She says it's difficult for even her to believe she got so deep into the drugs, prostitution and the lifestyle. "I wasn't raised like that. My mother did a hell of a job raising four kids. But once he took me out of town, that was the cutoff of anybody who loved me. I had to learn how to love him and depend on him."

In a way, she was brainwashed. She says he could make her believe that a carpet was blue even though she knew it was green. The drugs enabled her to get through being prostituted. "I medicated myself to deal with someone touching me."

Of course, the abuse wasn't limited to her. In Minnesota, he recruited some girls who'd been living in a trap house— an empty house where drugs were sold. They'd already been beaten up. "I told him they were too young, but he told me to shut up."

In 1996, after her abductor had been featured on the TV show *America's Most Wanted* his brother, who was with them, was arrested. He confessed, and their phones were tapped.

As usual, her abductor came up with an escape plan and headed out in one of their Cadillacs. "The next day, I packed up all the kids. That was my lifestyle for years—packing up the kids, taking care of the paperwork, going to the bank, getting money out because all this stuff was in my name. Everything: house, cars. It was never on him, but all on me. So if they were looking for him, they were looking for me. I didn't even know that I was in the lifestyle because I didn't grow up from that. I was so green. It went on for years. You mess up in a state, we pack up, we go."

They'd lived in thirty-two states until the day they were tracked down to a movie theater, surrounded, and arrested as soon as they walked out the doors. "We were supposed to be armed and dangerous. We had fake IDs, the whole nine yards." The man was extradited to another state and she was taken back to Nashville, her home town. "I'd never been in trouble a day in my life until October 19th, 1996." It's a day she'll never forget because it was a day before her birthday.

"I was fixing to go to jail for something that I didn't even realize I was in. But what they got me on was criminal impersonation and forgery because they saw all these different IDs with my name on them."

Released on her own recognizance after two weeks, Camille soon had a nervous breakdown. "I didn't know how to restart my life." Luckily, she says, her family rallied around her and helped her raise her kids. She found it hard and went to Knoxville because she knew where the guy had stashed money and drugs. She trusted someone to sell the drugs for her. "It was a big mess because it wasn't my lifestyle. I didn't know how to do it."

Camille could not break away from the life and got involved with another trafficker. When he crashed his car, she suffered severe eye and pelvis injuries. In another attempt to get clean, Camille went into a court-appointed two-year program but only lasted nine months before going back to the trafficker.

"Nobody even told me I was messed up the way that I was. The only thing I could think of was to use. I even went on a date on a walker. I needed the money so I could get high." A date? It was a client who hadn't realized she was so seriously hurt and told her she should heal up first. "But we still did whatever, so he was just as sick as I was."

Camille went through a number of temporary jobs. Friends who'd got out of the life tried repeatedly to rescue her, but she kept slipping back. "I was spiraling, spiraling, spiraling, trying to live on both sides of the fence." She wanted to be with her family, with her four kids and ten grandchildren. "I was there physically as far as money-wise, but I wasn't there mentally."

Her turning point came on Thanksgiving of 2018. Her youngest child's paternal grandfather had given them a house "because I helped take care of him through all this madness." She cooked turkey, ham, macaroni and cheese, and sweet potatoes—the whole Thanksgiving dinner—for family and friends. "Dope dealers still eat with their family and friends," she says. "And I was doing something nice for the ones that had burnt bridges and couldn't go home." But when she was out of the house on a drug run, one of the guests stole the turkey out of the oven and blamed it on the dog.

"For eight hours, I was on the phone calling people, telling them I'd made this big, fabulous dinner and somebody stole the turkey and blamed it on the dog."

When the person returned the next day, Camille couldn't hold back from attacking her. "It was like an out of body experience and I could see myself beating this person to a pulp, and I could feel it in my body where I wanted to kill her." If others hadn't pulled Camille off the woman, she might have killed the woman. "That was the day I knew I could no longer live like this. I never want to feel that in my body again."

Her friends who'd left the life contacted Empower Her Network in Atlanta, and they came to the rescue.

"It was a relief, a new beginning. After thirty-two years of wreckage, I needed to start being accountable and having responsibilities. So I needed to take my hands off the wheel and allow somebody in to help me. It was like I was crawling all over again until I could get on my feet and start walking and dictate what my life is supposed to be for me. I was no longer in bondage. I was free. I started caring about me, and it is the most beautiful journey I have ever been on. I'm joyous, happy, and free."

Camille completed the two-year program and is trying to mend her relationships with her kids. "I've always had an open channel with them, and they know about my life on the streets." She now has a condo, and after a lot of training, she has become a representative for the Empower Her Network organization, speaking on its behalf and facilitating groups.

"I want to be able to give back and help other women not go through the same things I have gone through. I want to be that advocate for women that want to get out of the lifestyle."

Camille even took a business class and started her own organization, Krystal Clear Foundation, helping women who are eighteen to twenty-five without a high school diploma get their GEDs. Once they have a GED, she helps them get into trades or certification programs.

What about a meaningful relationship with a man?

"I don't even have a boyfriend, and I'm not a bad looking woman. I need to just learn how to love myself more. If God wants me to have someone, then it will happen."

Considering the abuse she and her sister experienced at the hands of their stepfather and the sex trafficking that followed, what Camille has been able to overcome and accomplish is extraordinary—especially her mission to help other women.

Chapter 7

When Stepdads Step Up:
NFL Player Justin Pugh's Story

When a stepfather steps into the lives of children, it presents an entirely new set of challenges that can be a force for good—or evil. The family dynamic can be especially unsettling if a child's biological father passed away and he has strong memories and attachment.

Sadly, a considerable body of research highlights the downsides and dangers.

- Stepfamilies experience a higher level of mental disorders including separation anxiety disorder, major depressive disorder, and conduct disorder.

- Stepfathers invest less in the children who live with them.

- Stepchildren are more likely to have emotional and behavioral problems.

Of course, not all the data is bad, and stepdads can play a critical role in steering a child through the trauma of having lost a parent.

- Boys may find a source of companionship and support as they look to the stepfather as a major role model.

- A close, supportive relationship between stepfather and stepson has been found to alleviate behavioral problems as well as increase social competence in preadolescent boys.

Stepfathers often find themselves in a delicate balancing act as they try to establish a meaningful connection with the child while respecting the child's loyalty to their biological father's memory. A caring stepfather can provide emotional support and stability, helping to heal emotional wounds. They can be a positive role model, offering guidance and mentorship while contributing to the financial stability of the household, ensuring that the child's basic needs are met. On top of that, they can introduce children to new experiences and opportunities, thereby broadening their horizons and enriching their lives.

Successfully integrating into a blended family requires effort and patience. A stepfather who is committed to fostering a harmonious family dynamic can help create a sense of unity and belonging among all family members. Through encouragement and positive reinforcement, a stepfather can boost the child's self-esteem and confidence. Knowing that there is someone who believes in them can be instrumental in their personal growth and development.

The following story about NFL offensive guard Justin Pugh is a perfect example of the immense value a good stepfather brings to the blended family and a boy's development.

Justin's Story

Justin is as tough as they come. But his soft side is on display when he openly talks about his parents' divorce when he was a young boy, the death of his dad, and how his stepdad helped mold him into the man he has become today.

Justin, who rose to prominence when the New York Giants selected him with the nineteenth overall pick in the 2013 NFL draft, told me, "The person that was there for me the most was my stepfather. I wouldn't be here without his guidance. It's been a good ending to a very bad scenario."

Growing up in the suburbs of Philadelphia, Justin's mom and dad, David and Carolyn Pugh, divorced when he was five or six, and he was too young to understand what was happening. His father worked for NASCAR, traveling across the country selling souvenirs out of a large trailer. Justin and his sister, Jenna, kept in touch by sending videos telling him they loved him. For a month in the summer, they joined their dad on the road, helping sell souvenirs, replica cars, and shirts, and he'd visit them at Christmas.

"He had the best gifts. I would get an authentic jersey or a PlayStation video game that was big at the time. That was his way of making up for not being around so much. I'd give my mom a hard time for not getting us more. Looking back, I can see she was suffering in silence, putting up with a lot," Justin said.

Before starting eighth grade, Justin worked for a month that summer for his dad, who'd transitioned into a job involving burying telephone cables. "I hated it, although I really learned the value of hard work and the importance of getting an education. My mom, who was a schoolteacher, always harped about education, and after that summer, I went home and told her, 'I'm going to college. I'm getting my degree. I'm always going to have that piece of paper to fall back on.'"

While working with his dad in North Carolina, Justin says he kept asking him, "Why don't you move back up north to be close to Jenna and me?" Justin didn't understand why he was living so far away, which meant he could only see his father two or three times a year. "And still to this day, I have no idea. I never got a straight answer. Maybe there was guilt or shame that he lost his job and wasn't able to provide the life he thought he should."

Meanwhile, Justin's mom, Carolyn, had remarried and they had moved in with his stepdad, Frank Gavaghan, and two stepbrothers. His stepbrother Shaun was ten years older than him and Michael was eight years his senior. "That's when I had some great role models. They kind of took me in."

Justin admits he had a rebellious streak and was surprised when his stepdad came to the school one day to get him out of detention. The reason was shocking. His dad, at the age of forty-six, had suffered a massive heart attack at work and died. "I'd never encountered death before. You don't think at thirteen that it's real, that someone could die. He'd made all these promises about moving back. You build your father up to be this mythical figure, and then before it could happen, he passes away. It was a shock to my whole being."

His stepdad, who'd lost his own father a few years earlier, stepped up bigtime. He was a rock. "My dad passing away was a tragedy I had to overcome, but I had this man that was there in my life, that was a father figure. I never felt like I didn't have a dad. If you don't have that person that steps in and fills that void, you're going to be at a loss. My stepdad was there, so I've had it all. He was the one that really comforted me and got me through it."

According to Justin, Frank Gavaghan was a disciplinarian who taught him the value of hard work and set an example by going to work at 5:00 a.m. every day as a carpenter before becoming a project manager for the multinational construction company, Skanska.

"When he spoke, you listened. He was very tough from the point of view of doing chores like mowing the lawn and not speaking back to your mother. Do the right thing. No elbows on the table. That kind of thing. And I needed that structure. I didn't know I needed it. I probably hated it at the time." Furthermore, he says he was "a little punk" who'd tell Frank, "You're not my dad. You can't tell me what to do." Words I'm sure most, if not all, stepdads have heard.

Tough love from Frank put an end to Justin's temper tantrums. Frank was also an ice hockey coach. Both of Justin's older brothers played the sport, so it was inevitable he would too. He inherited his brothers' equipment until he outgrew it, and because of the cost factor, he was encouraged in seventh grade to transition to football. "The competition, the violence, suited me even more. Football was the kind of outlet for that side of me."

And besides, he says, Frank "always joked that I skated like I had a refrigerator strapped to my back. I wasn't the fastest, but I had a knack for aggression."

Justin never looked back. In high school, he started as a raw six feet two inches, two hundred pounder and left as a man-child who was four inches taller and sixty pounds heavier than when he was as a freshman. And with a scholarship to play for Syracuse University. At college, he says they'd break players into separate groups of those who either wanted to be recruited by the NFL as a defensive lineman or offensive lineman. Justin wanted to be a defensive lineman, but Frank had other ideas. "He wasn't always on a soapbox, going on and on, but when he had something to say, he would let you know—this is the decision we're going with. He grabbed me and insisted I was an offensive lineman. He was an ice hockey coach and a good judge of athleticism. I started leaning toward the offensive line at camps, and it ended up being a good decision."

Justin played as an offensive lineman for Syracuse and throughout his professional career, and he gives his stepfather credit for instilling in him the motivation to work hard.

Justin may well have been a protector as early as the age of six, and he grew up with the six or seven guys he became friends with at that age. "They're all a bit smaller than me and Jewish, except for me. We would joke that they were the smartest guys in the room, and they'd picked the biggest kid in first grade to be friends with them and protect them. They did the talking and I'd back them up."

Of course, Justin is too modest. He's plenty smart. He fulfilled a promise to his mom, a schoolteacher for thirty-five years, to get his degree in finance, and after getting that degree, he often went back to talk to her class.

Frank Gavaghan attended all of Justin's college games, home and away, except one. Sadly, his biological father never had the same opportunity. "My dad never saw me play football, so I don't know how he'd respond to what I'm doing right now. I kind of daydream about what that relationship would be like. At the same time, I'm very fortunate to have the family in place that I do, that took me under their wing."

Justin's professional career began on July 25, 2013 when the New York Giants signed him to a four-year contract. Family and friends joined the wild celebrations, a family he says is healthily competitive. "My sister is the toughest chick you'll ever meet. She had to deal with my brothers and me. She can dish it out with the best of them to this day. And my older brothers taught me about competition. Everything in our family is a competition."

That includes cooking, golf, beach volleyball, spike ball, whiffle ball, and even a family Olympics every Fourth of July. "I was always striving for the acceptance of my older brothers. I wanted to impress them so much, to fit in. They took me from a little spoiled brat to somewhat of a less spoiled brat."

The whole family was supportive of his football career. When his sister and two cousins were in high school, they started a group called The Pugh Crew, and everyone in the group who attended a game was given a T-shirt. At his final college game, he had two hundred and fifty supporters from his mom's, dad's, and stepdad's families. "It's a great family infrastructure that has really carried through to this day."

In March 2018, Justin and his girlfriend, Angela Viscount, made the tough decision to move away from family and friends when he was signed by the Arizona Cardinals. Since Justin and Angela married in April 2022, his father-in-law has been another male figure who has greatly impacted his life. "He's become another father to me, and I call him all the time for advice." Unfortunately, after a durable decade in the league starting 199 games and playing across 120, his fifth and final season for the Cardinals was cut short in the fall of 2022 when he suffered a torn ACL. A year later he returned to the Giants' roster.

Justin says that Angela has been his rock, and their first child, a girl named Josephine "Joie" James Pugh, made her debut on January 21, 2024. "Now I get to be a father, and I get to instill in her all those things that my family has instilled in me. I couldn't be more excited about raising a child with Angela. I knew she was the one that was perfect for me. I wanted my children to be half of her."

Justin discovered he was going to become a dad when he arrived home one day to find Angela crying in the kitchen in front of fifteen pregnancy tests and baby onesies while a Jordan Davis song about fatherhood played in the background. "I was in shock trying to analyze all this," Justin said. "It was such an unbelievable moment." Even Justin teared up a bit. "You start thinking about the responsibility that's now on your plate. So that's another adventure."

Justin sees some good examples to follow with how teammates (as well as his mom) have raised their daughters. "I'm going to have a learning curve with a newborn baby and to make sure I'm comfortable holding her and changing diapers. That's one thing I haven't done a lot. I'm sure I'll get competitive and tell my wife I can change the diaper faster than she can. One thing I think about a lot is being there for my child and providing the best life she could ever imagine. That's a father's dream."

Inevitably, the conversation turns back to Justin's own biological dad. "I broke down crying uncontrollably at my sister's wedding because it's an occasion when her father was supposed to be there to walk her down the aisle."

His advice to young men: "Have conversations. Don't be afraid to talk about your emotions. Remember that with social media, your reputation will follow you a lot longer than it once did, so treat people with respect. That's something I wish I had done early on in life." And also, "Shoot for the moon and be a nice person."

Justin talks frankly about resenting the fact that his dad left this world before he could have a real conversation with him and how he felt about his dad not being around for him. Nevertheless, he keeps his dad close: He has a tattoo that is a copy of his dad's Navy dog tags to ensure that his dad is always with him.

He will be the first to say that the person who has always been with him is the stepdad who took over the role of dad and more than filled that role.

Chapter 8

Becoming the Father
He Never Had

Michael Callahan's rocky experience growing up with three fathers turned him off becoming a father himself—until he met the right woman. Now that he's a dad, he's determined to give his son a better childhood than he had.

Michael is my brother, the oldest of six kids. He only met his birth father twice in his entire life, and he's gone through the divorce of both stepdads. Growing up with Michael, I never thought much about the differences between us, but as I became an adult and had a child of my own, I wondered what it must have been like being the only child out of the six of us who did not have a sibling sharing the same biological mother and father. What was it like to watch his siblings with their biological father but not have a relationship with his own? And what was it like to not have anyone else in the family who truly understood his situation?

When I decided to write this book, Michael was the first person I reached out to, hoping he would be willing to tell his story and talk about the challenges he faced. I was thankful when he agreed because now I can truly understand what it was like for him and why it is so important for him to be such a strong father figure in his son's life.

Dad Number One

Michael's birth dad, also named Michael, met our mom, Joanne, when they were about eighteen. Many years later, Michael says he discovered that his dad hadn't stuck around for more than a couple of months. He was young and immature.

Michael didn't see or hear much of his dad. The first contact was when he was between seven and eight years old. "My grandmother, my dad's mom, put me on the phone against my mom's wishes, and I talked to him for a few minutes." The second time was when Michael was around eighteen years old, and they arranged to meet at an IHOP restaurant. Following his dad to a seat at the counter, Michael noticed they had a similar physical build. "He's got a wide frame like me."

"You have my eyes," Michael said to his dad.

His dad replied, "No, boy. You have mine."

"It's a pretty crazy story," Michael said, "although kind of sad because he only said a few things to me."

Michael's third connection was around the age of twenty, by which time he knew about his father's long struggle with drug addiction. His dad had become very involved in the church and had graduated from a Bible college. "I remember it was important to him. I went there to congratulate him, and we took a picture in the parking lot."

His dad's struggles with drugs began at a very young age and at a time when prescription drugs were relatively easy to get. "He was kind of wild and crazy and experimenting with everything that the seventies had to offer." When Michael's grandfather committed suicide, his dad went into a downward spiral. "He went off the deep end and got into more drugs after his dad killed himself. He walked through the police tape and saw that. You can imagine how that affected a seventeen-year-old boy. After that, I think all bets were off. He was just a bit more than mildly self-destructive."

Michael saw his dad one last time—after his sudden death when Michael was twenty three years old. "The first feeling I had was that I'd lost the chance to get to know that person. There was no more time. I felt helpless, like there was nothing I could do. I'd just fall in line and do whatever I was supposed to do. I wasn't ready for that call. I thought I'd have more time, I really did."

Ironically, the news came when he was in a sales company's motivational meeting. "I had to run out and take the call in the middle of a positivity session. There's never really an appropriate setting, but it added to the shock."

He says he moved into "handle it" mode. He went to his grandmother's house, where his dad had lived, and was told to take any of his dad's possessions he wanted. "I went through his things in his room. It was a really quiet, really eerie ten to fifteen minutes of my life." He found some birthday cards, which made him suspect he might have a sister somewhere, and he read his dad's journals. "He had a lot of struggles. I could tell he was in a lot of pain." He came away with the journals, a pool cue, and a Bible.

As next of kin, he needed to go to the morgue, so he went with his father's mother and grandmother to identify the body of the dad he never really knew. "We pulled down the sheet. I didn't know what to do, and they said, 'Say goodbye or whatever you want to do.' I gave him a kiss on the forehead, and it was cold. Weird. Just a shame, a shame."

Sitting in the front row at the funeral was an odd, awkward moment. "I met a lot of people and should probably reach out to them and learn more about them." There were people from his father's side of the family and people he grew up with as well as a leader in his church group who told him some stories about his dad. "It was just condolences from a lot of people I didn't know. It was a bizarre scenario. I wasn't ready to process it."

Michael had to handle the sale of his dad's possessions: an old condo that was trashed, which he got an investor to help fix up and sell, an old van, and two cars. He found a connection to his dad in a trunk, a sales kit from a marketing company called Excel. Michael unknowingly followed in his footsteps, signing up at a similar company and selling similar products. "So apparently my father was in Excel a long, long time ago. I thought that was kind of cute. I've always been in sales, and I was told my dad was a really great insurance agent before he had his troubles later in life."

Dad Number Two

Michael's second dad was Dave Knight who married my mom and together had two children, my brother David Jr. and me.

"I don't remember thinking that Dave was my dad," Michael said, "but I have pretty strong memories thinking he was a father figure. I have positive memories of you guys being very small and him always being nice to me. I just remember thinking, well, I guess my dad's not here. I'll work that out later. I never really got a whole lot of later though."

Dad Number Three

Mom divorced Dave, met Jack, and eventually married him and had three more children, Matthew, Chelsea, and Autumn. Michael was six when she introduced him to the family. "I remember her taking me into the garage and explaining that I needed to start calling him dad," Michael said. "It felt weird to me. I never thought of referring to Dave as Dad. Maybe I did, but I always knew he was Dave, kind of a cool stepdad." Michael went along with calling Jack his dad and says that for a lot of years, at least a decade, we were "a pretty regular family, waiting at the bottom of the stairs at Christmas, videotaping. A kind of normal upbringing."

Michael remembers visiting Dave for a few weeks in the summer. "It was like a vacation for me. I knew how much it meant to DJ to go see his dad."

Michael was around twenty-two years old when Mom and Jack divorced. At the time, he was out of the house living in his first apartment. "That's the point when the marriage fell apart, and I was just trying to shield all the little kids from this weird shit that's happening," Michael said. He went through a period of personal growth in his twenties. "I would always say I had a normal upbring because I felt bad for some of my siblings that were at more tender ages when some of these major things happened. I used to say that Autumn [the youngest] and I were the least affected, and I think that maybe that was a defense mechanism for me."

Michael's experience with the death of a dad he barely knew and two other dads getting divorced turned him off on the thought of becoming a father himself. "For a lot of my twenties, I was on record saying, 'I'm not having kids.' I just didn't want some of the things that I saw happen to us. I didn't want to contribute to that. Because I didn't have a good role model, I thought I probably just wouldn't have kids. If you mess that up, you can create a real problem for society."

He added a qualifier. "Well, Jack was a fine stepdad, but I saw him disconnect with all of the children when they became teenagers, and now he doesn't have a relationship with any of us that he raised. My point is that I don't have a 100 percent good father figure that I look to."

His attitude was that there had already been three Michael Callahans: his grandfather, his father, and himself. He felt that most things were good in threes, so he should be the end of the line. "Let's do the trilogy. I'll be the last. End on a high note. It's a little dramatic, but kind of sad."

That attitude changed completely when he met Jessica, his future wife. "It showed me that I wanted to have a child and take that challenge. When you meet the right person, you think it's the most important thing you can do if you can really pour your heart into that and be good at that. When I found out Jess was pregnant, I was super excited."

He and Jessica discovered the baby's gender when they were at a restaurant. "I started screaming. I'm yelling at everyone, 'I'm having a boy. You hear that? I'm having a boy.' There's a video of me jumping up and down. Something kicks in . . . it must be nature, like this is the most important thing. A tremendous sense of duty came from deep within me."

Michael now feels that unlike his fathers, he can be a role model. "I have a lot to give back. I have a lot to share. It's not hard to improve on where we came from."

He wants to have his son, Michael IV, benefit from his experience. "I think he's really smart, kind, and funny, and I want him to leave the world a better place than he finds it. I'm going to tell him to do his best. You're gonna fall down but get back up."

What has Michael learned? He says that although there was instability in our family, Mom was a rock, and wonderful, but that there's only so much one person can do. With broken families an epidemic in the United States, he advocates for the traditional family unit. "I respect single mothers and I respect different sorts of families, but a child needs a mother and father. That's the ideal situation. If you find the right person, you can overcome where you come from. If you find the right person, you should try to keep that marriage and build a nuclear family."

Reflecting on the lack of a relationship with his father, who died when both were so young, he says, "You never know when you won't get to speak to someone again, so if you have strained relationship with any close relative, talk to them. If you only get one side of a story, that's a shame. Talk to that person even if it's painful, awkward, and uncomfortable. Reach out to that person, because you never know what the future holds."

Michael knows what it's like to grow up disappointed with three fathers and is determined that his son always feels comfort, knowing how much he loves him.

Chapter 9

From Cult Victim
to Loving Father of Three

There are thousands of cults in America today and millions of devotees. Expert opinion differs on just how many there are. You're probably familiar with those that have grabbed the headlines over the years for a variety of negative and truly horrific reasons.

Say "Waco" and most people think of the Branch Davidians led by David Koresh (who saw himself as the Messiah) and the 1993 FBI standoff at their compound in Waco, Texas, which ended in a raging fire that killed seventy-six members. Charles Manson and the Manson Family's sensational 1968 Tate-LaBianca murders have been widely documented. And it's interesting to note that Manson grew up in an abusive household.

Maybe you've heard of Jim Jones, who led 909 members of his cult, the Peoples Temple, in a mass suicide at "Jonestown" in the jungle of Guyana in 1974. Or you might have heard of the Heaven's Gate group, who believed that God, Jesus, and the angels were part of a superior race of extraterrestrials. In 1997, thirty-nine of its members took a lethal mixture of phenobarbital and vodka expecting a spacecraft hidden behind the Hale-Bopp comet to take them to a higher existence. In 2017, a group called NXIVM (pronounced NEX-ee-um), which positioned itself as a self-help organization, was revealed to have recruited women who thought they were joining a sisterhood of sorts. But it ended up being a sex cult.

As cult survivors' advocate Lida Magdelena says, "Cults, by their very nature, often manipulate and exploit their members, leaving deep scars that can affect survivors long after they've left the cult. The psychological and emotional issues faced by individuals who grow up in a cult are unique and complex."

A study in the journal *Traumatology* spells out the issues. "Survivors of destructive cults report a number of symptoms resulting from the aftereffects of traumatic experiences of physical, sexual, emotional, mental and spiritual abuse which include depression, anxiety, panic attacks, flashbacks, nightmares, guilt, self-blame, anger, shame, humiliation, and a variety of other distressing emotions."

Peter's Story

One well-adjusted survivor is Peter Gronvall, a loving father of three, which is a remarkable statement to make considering his own childhood.

Peter's father became enamored with an extreme religious group, which he says turned into a cult, and Peter's upbringing was a strange mix of two worlds. During the week, he went to school like most kids, but on weekends and during the summer, he was trapped in a compound where he was abused physically and emotionally while his parents, Kal and Kathleen Gronvall, turned a blind eye.

It all began when Peter was two years old, the second in what would become a family of nine children, five girls and four boys. His dad was a high school basketball and track coach in Mankato, Minnesota, a typical outdoorsman with many friends. Peter remembers him as a smiling, cordial father. Then, he says, his dad was seduced into joining a small counter-establishment religious group.

The religious beliefs of the cult, The Disciples of the Lord Jesus Christ, was originally a strange brew of Eastern mythology and fundamentalist Christianity. It was led by a Hindu-born Christian from India, Rama Behera, who later changed his name to Samanta Roy and the group's name to the Samanta Roy Institute of Science and Technology. Eventually, after morphing into an obsession with Judaism, Rama Behera changed his name again to Avraham Cohen.

The cult leader, whatever his name, ruled with an iron fist. "Our parents' authority was undermined by this crazy narcissist, a psychopath who broke down traditional family values," Peter said. "We grew up being constructively abandoned by our parents into this hardcore fundamentalist hellfire and brimstone cult. The conditions were unspeakable."

At home in Mankato, Peter's family had friends and neighbors. "It was known that my family was different, but nobody really stepped on our toes." They had no TV or radio. Peter and his siblings went to school but stood out because of their appearance. The boys had buzz cuts and basic work clothes—collared shirts and long pants. The girls had long hair and were modestly dressed in full-length dresses so their legs were not exposed. "It was a form of humiliation to break down any vanity, identity, or self-worth."

Middle and high school years are difficult enough socially for kids, but being dressed differently and being away at the cult every weekend made their lives very difficult. "We saw how other people lived. We sneaked to a friend's house to watch TV or to 7-Eleven to get a candy bar. We lived in both worlds."

After school on Friday, the family drove six or seven hours, regardless of the weather, to the cult's compound, a farm in Shawano near Green Bay, Wisconsin, to spend the weekend in worship and hard labor. People slept in their sleeping bags on concrete floors or in their cars. At early Saturday morning religious meetings, families were split up and divided by gender for several hours of songs, Bible readings, and a fiery rant from the cult leader.

"This horrible monster would tear into us with his fire and brimstone ravings. We're all doomed. We're all going to hell. He terrorized people for having worldly thoughts or wanting to be anywhere but in the cult. It was an environment of fear, and I don't think it's what men and women signed up for, but brainwashing took over."

After the meeting, adults and children were sent to work in the fields or construction on barns and buildings under very unsafe working conditions. They'd be given one meal and either attend a night meeting or work into the small hours until a brief rest before a Sunday morning meeting. They'd get back home to Mankato exhausted, beaten up by the abuse, hard labor, and terrible living conditions. It was a tough, grueling routine.

"We'd drag ourselves out of bed and go back to school on Monday morning, but you were still a kid in a cult with a bad haircut and really awful clothes who'd missed out on all the normal things that kids do with their friends on the weekend. We were living two lives, which was tough. I was being a kid trying to fit in and have friendships. School was a sanctuary for me coming off those brutal weekends. I loved being around my classmates and made the most of it, but I had this secret horrible part of my life that I was embarrassed about."

The worst time for Peter, he says, began when he was six and forced to spend summer months at the camp, separated from his parents. "They gave me up because it was demanded I stay there. I slept on cardboard. I drank out of puddles. I was viciously cattle-prodded and beaten with electric cords. I was tormented by one man who took a lot of joy beating me up and locking me in dark rooms. It was a full hostage situation, so you can imagine how sick that was. I survived as best I could."

Peter missed the smell of his home, sleeping in his own bed, and not seeing his family until the weekend. "I never lost sight of the fact that this was not right. You're in this twisted nightmare and you make the most of it. You find a way to find hope and you keep going."

The cult leader and his deputies did not treat all the families equally. Some were favorites and got off lightly. Others were viciously attacked, and the Gronvall family was one of those because, Peter says, he and his siblings had self-will and light in their eyes. His dad, however, was a true believer. "Unfortunately, my dad was one of the people who went all in and ceded his children and his own life and happiness to this psychopath who ended up destroying families. We saw a grown man give up control of his life and allow these things to calcify and increase in magnitude. We never felt like we had a protector."

Children at the compound were treated harshly in front of their parents and their friends. "Our lives were full of anguish and dread of the physical abuse, not knowing what was going to happen next."

Even as a middle schooler, Peter recognized the cult's way of life was "horrifically wrong" and that his dad had been duped. "I pleaded with him to look around. He'd lost his friends. He was a well-liked person, a beloved teacher who lost his job because he was evangelizing to his students. He alienated himself from his parents, and my mom did the same thing. He became this lifeless, pathetic person. He doubled down on the cult because he believed it was the way of the Lord and the way to get to heaven."

Peter saw the cult leader as "a monster who was followed as a sort of beacon when in fact he was the Antichrist." Obedience and subservience were demanded as if they were virtues. "It's about as caustic and toxic as anything you can imagine when parents who are supposed to be the ultimate protectors are brainwashed into abandoning their children and allow things to happen to them in their presence."

As they grew older, Peter and his siblings developed the tightest of bonds and were a source of strength, humor, and resourcefulness for each other, traits that continue as adults. "We all kind of parented each other. It became a symbiotic group. We found joy and strength with each other."

Peter's break from the cult started through academic achievement. Without a TV or radio in the home, he became a voracious reader. He did so well at school, he got a full ride academic scholarship to the University Of Minnesota, and although he wanted to run away, he continued to visit the cult on weekends to stay close to his younger siblings. "I was being treated better because I was physically bigger and could resist my abusers."

Accepted by both Harvard and Yale Law School on the same day, Peter felt it was his cue to move east and start his own life. After graduating from Yale, he practiced law with prestigious firms in Washington, DC, during which time mutual friends introduced him to his wife to be, who was graduating from George Washington University and luckily, he says, came from a wonderful traditional family. When they married, he was walked down the aisle by two sisters and one brother. His mom and other siblings were still trapped in the cult and could not attend.

Eventually, all of Peter's siblings escaped from the cult and are now thriving professionals. His mom got out too, as did other people, since the conditions continued to deteriorate. "Her children were adults, having children of their own, and she really needed to be with her family," he said. "My sisters get all the credit. They picked her up and gave her a soft landing, and she got to be reunited with her mother, our grandmother. She emancipated herself, and we received her with open arms. And she's basking in the glow of her many grandchildren."

As far as Peter knows, his father is still in the cult. He has had no contact with him since the late 1990s. "I don't even remember the last time I heard his voice."

What would he do if they reconnected? "I don't really have anything to say to him. It was really tragic to have this wonderful family and throw it away and put us through these decades of absolute hell. It's so pathetic. But I have come to peace with it. There's no tension or conflict in me."

His advice to young men who find themselves without a father or caught in a complicated relationship? "Find a mentor. People are good by nature and want to help. Maybe it's a coach, high school administrator, or even a neighbor."

Today, Peter has a successful business career, teaches at Georgetown Law School, and has a great outlook on life. "I have this almost pathological optimism. Mindfulness is something that I've practiced since I was a little kid when I didn't even know that that's what I was doing."

His focus is to make sure his children have a strikingly different childhood than the one he had. "When I knew I was becoming a father, it was like my life was starting over. I was probably craving fatherhood because I was craving childhood. To be a father was my way of breaking the cycle."

Peter vividly recalls observing his oldest son when he was four. "I was in complete awe watching him in the backyard holding a butterfly. It took my breath away because I remember what I was going through at that age."

The most important thing he wants to instill in his kids is a feeling of safety and security. He wants to give them a first-class education and the confidence to be curious, ask questions, and make mistakes. He says that his three children are all kind, empathetic, and conversational. "I have a list of stories that bring tears to my eyes seeing my children engage with adults across the spectrum. It's like emotional safety. Coming from the depths of trauma and poverty, I'm mindful and grateful seeing them experience my best version of a good childhood."

The son of a man lost to a cult is determined that his children will never suffer anything similar. His children will always feel his unconditional love.

Chapter 10

How the Death of a Father Shapes a Son's Life

Inescapably, the death of a father has a profound effect on children. You might be surprised to learn that, according to the latest US Census Bureau statistics, nearly 11 percent of children lose their dads before the age of fifteen. The consequences can be dire and endure for years.

There can be an impact on offspring's health later in life, increased alcohol consumption, depression, mental health issues, PTSD, suicide, and less success in education and work environments. Research also shows the negative effects are often much worse for boys than for girls.

Mortality Risk

Researchers in Denmark, Sweden, and Finland identified nearly one hundred and ninety thousand individuals who had lost a parent between the age of six months and eighteen years and found they had a 50 percent higher death rate well into early adulthood. The risk was even higher if the parent's death was unnatural. Study authors stated, "Given that increased mortality probably only represents the tip of the iceberg of the adverse effects of early bereavement, these findings highlight the need to provide long-term health and social support to bereaved children."

In a study that followed children for up to forty years, Scandinavian researchers also found that those who experienced parental death before they reached eighteen were more likely to commit suicide, especially those whose parent passed while they were under the age of six.

In another study of nearly one million people, published in the *Journal of Epidemiology and Community Health,* about 12 percent had lost a father by age thirty-one. Those who lost a parent before the age of twenty-one had higher odds of a hospital admission for mental health issues than those who lost a parent after age thirty. Men were 70 percent more likely to be hospitalized, with the most common reasons being substance abuse disorders and intentional self-harm. The same study found that losing a parent before the age of twenty-one was also linked with fewer years of schooling, lower annual earnings, and more periods of unemployment.

Education Challenges

The absence of a father figure can impact a child's educational attainment and professional success. They may struggle with motivation, discipline, and self-esteem, making it more challenging to excel in school and their careers. Multiple studies show that kids who have lost a parent are more than twice as likely than nonbereaved kids to show impairments in functioning at school and at home, even seven years later.

My case history in this chapter is personal. It's my father-in-law, who overcame the challenges of losing his father at an early age and went on to be a guiding force in many lives.

Gerald's Story

Gerald Truman was born in 1943 into a large Italian family living in Campbell, Ohio, a suburb of Youngstown, a city renowned for its steel industry. At his sixth birthday party, he was given the worst possible news: His dad had passed away. It was March 31, 1949. Two days earlier, his dad had called Gerald and his older brother, Tony, into the room in their house where he lay in bed and told them to take care of their mother and that everything would be okay.

The birthday party was at the home of Gerald's godparents, Andrew and Theresa Profancik. He remembers his mom arriving at the party and telling him his dad had passed. The rest of the day was a blur in which he felt confused and overwhelmed.

"At six years old, you don't anticipate stuff like that, and you don't really know what to do," Gerald told me.

The wake and funeral were huge events lasting for at least two days and attended by more than five hundred people. Gerald remembers people shoving coins into his pockets as birthday gifts and in an effort to cheer him up. It was a difficult time. In addition to Tony, he had a brother Terry, two years younger, and his mom was three and a half months pregnant with his sister, Diane.

Gerald's father had worked in the Briar Hill Steel Mill in Youngstown, and his mother worked in a downtown shoe repair shop. "He used to take us in the car to pick up my mother, and he'd always stop at a candy store to get candy for us."

About the time after his father's passing, Gerald said, "It was tough, but you try to make the best of it." They were helped by his father's four sisters, who all lived within a quarter mile of their home. The male influence in Gerald's life became his grandfather, Dominic Trumfio. "I spent a lot of time with my grandfather, my dad's dad, the Italian side of the family. He lived down the street from us."

Every Sunday, the family got together at the grandparents' house and visited with all the aunts. "So they all knew what we were doing, what was going on." And the aunts kept him and his siblings on the straight and narrow. "They made sure that we walked the chalk line."

Financially, it was difficult for a single mom with four kids. His mom's friends who lived nearby kept an eye on them when she worked her new job as a waitress. Gerald and his brother pitched in and worked numerous jobs from a young age. Gerald's first job, at the age of eight, was cutting neighbors' grass using a push mower.

By the time he was thirteen, Gerald would go to work as soon as he arrived home from school. Four days a week he cleaned a pizza shop. On Saturdays, he worked at a gas station owned by one of his mother's friends. It wasn't easy. He left home at 6:00 a.m., caught two buses, arrived at work at about 8:30 a.m., and spent the entire day washing cars. That night, from 10:00 p.m. until about 1:00 a.m., he and his older brother delivered bundles of newspapers to locations for people to pick up and take to households. Back home, they'd get ready for mass.

"Every Sunday, no ifs, ands, or buts, we had to get dressed up and go to church." Gerald said there was always something in the gospel that provided values for life.

After that, it was back to work. They'd wash and polish several cars. "We just did it. Every penny we made we gave to my mother."

Displaying an entrepreneurial spirit, Gerald scavenged bike parts from the local scrapyard and built complete bikes that he sold for five or six dollars. "It was just anything to make a dollar so we could survive."

Despite the heavy workload, Gerald was able to find some time for fun. He and his brother played baseball—T-ball, Little League, and Pony League. "My mother was at every game my brothers and I played, but we didn't have much time for sports, except in the summertime when we didn't have to go to school."

There were four schools with their own parks in Campbell, but they also had to keep watch over their younger siblings when their mother was working. Sometimes for several weeks in the summer, the kids stayed with their grandfather's sister and her sons in Geneva, Ohio, and walked or hitchhiked to the beach at Lake Erie. But first there was work to do. His cousins had a bar, and Gerald had to clean it before he could do anything else.

Summing up the impact of all that work, starting at a young age, Gerald said, "By the time I was fifty, I was ready to retire because I'd been working since I was eight years old."

Having family live in close proximity was a major advantage. "You could have all the friends in the world, but you really need the family. They stuck by us, and it was good. They helped a lot." The church helped too, and Gerald went to parochial school for eight years.

About 1956, a man entered his mother's life. "She worked at the restaurant, and he used to be there every night. And the next thing we come to find out is they're gonna get married." He was fourteen and his brother was sixteen. His mom and John Petko married the following year. His new stepdad was a union glazer (glass cutter) who made good money and provided financial and emotional support to the entire family. It was tough, though, for Gerald and his brothers Tony and Terry to have another male in the house.

Gerald met his future wife, Helen, when he was in tenth grade at the public high school, and they quickly became inseparable. "We went to the prom and did everything together all the time." He was seventeen when he graduated and drove out to California, where he lived with Helen's sister and brother-in-law while seeking work. "But it didn't pan out because I was too young."

Returning to Ohio, he and Helen continued dating and married three years later when he was twenty and she was twenty-one. He wanted to work on cars and open a gas station. He worked at a Sunoco gas station and had the opportunity to take it over, but the guy in charge was running it into the ground. On top of that, customers were difficult, and he thinks he might well have punched them out if he'd taken over the gas station. "I couldn't take the bologna from those guys."

Instead of operating a gas station, he went to work in the aluminum factory where they made frames and screen doors. He was also going to school to study refrigeration. In 1961, he applied for a job in Washington, DC, scored very high on a test, and after about a year was selected with a start date of

July 1963. They got married the following October and he got a waiver on military service because he was working a vital job in the government printing office. The original plan was to become a machinist, but because he passed an academic test, they gave him a five-year apprenticeship in the composing area, proofreading and setting type.

Did he like it? "No. I learned to like it, though. There are a lot of things I didn't like that I learned to like. It was too good of a job to turn down, and I learned how to work hard to advance myself."

He and Helen had a nice apartment, and in January of 1965, their first child, Karen, was born. "I was very close to my grandfather, and he came down to see us. He wanted to be sure he knew where I lived." His grandfather had strong traditional family values that he wasn't slow to preach. "He emphasized very clearly that I had to work and make money for my family and that my wife should have the ability to stay home with the kids. So it all worked out for the best, four kids later."

Having children, of course, was a lifechanging experience. "We had the two girls within a year, and we never went anywhere without them. Sometimes we might go to a dance and get someone to watch them, but very seldom. No matter what we did, they always came with us. If we went down to the ocean, they came—crib and canopy and all the rest of the stuff."

He even accumulated vacation time so they could take a thirty-one-day road trip to California. "It was wonderful. We had a ball. The best thing we ever did. Even the drive. We had a station wagon, and the girls and our oldest son, Jerry, who was a year and a half or two years old. The kids loved seeing different parts of the country."

Family life was all-important. "My work kept wanting to promote me and change my hours from nine to six thirty." He declined the promotion because he liked getting home by 3:30 or 4:00. "Helen would have dinner ready, and I wanted to spend time with the kids, take them to the pool, that kind of thing. There are people that work in the government hierarchy that are nuts. Their dinners are at ten o'clock at night. The Bureau of the Mint, for instance, might want you to come to a meeting at seven o'clock at night. Not me."

Gerald coached baseball for forty years at DeMatha High School (an all-boys school both of his sons, Jerry and Matt, graduated from), followed by Greenbelt, College Park, Prince George's Community College, and the American Legion. Gerald never accepted any payment for coaching because it was his passion.

The motivation to coach, he says, was to help kids succeed and go from being unable to even throw a ball to first base to throwing rockets or watch a kid make a catch requiring diving for the ball, something he'd taught him how to do without getting hurt. He laid down rules and believed in keeping to them. "When I said something, I meant it. These are the rules. This is what you're supposed to do. This is what you gotta do. And I wanted to see them grow, be responsible for their actions, and not rely on their parents all the time."

He'd call a kid's home and insist on speaking to the kid, not the parent. "A lot of parents would come to me to tell their kids something because they couldn't talk to them. I never had that problem with mine."

What were the most important values he wanted to instill in his children? First, he wanted to teach them the value of self-sufficiency. Second and third, he wanted them to value being responsible for their actions and being polite to people. "I taught them that when you walk into somebody's house, I don't care who it is, your aunt or friends or anybody, you always walk up and say hi. And when you leave their house, you tell 'em you're leaving. My wife and I thought it was very important that they do that, to have respect, and it grew on them. And I like to see parents today do that. Their job is not to be a friend but a parent."

He says he primarily learned values from his mother. She attended all his sports events, and he followed in her footsteps, whether his kids were in gymnastics, dancing, softball, baseball, or football. How did his mom do it when she was under so much stress to provide? "She was always able to put food on the table. But also, you learned how to do things yourself, how to repair things, how to cook." His grandfather, too, played a meaningful role. Gerald would spend thirty to forty-five minutes most evenings with him and play games of skill.

His grandfather never just let him win, and he's the same way with his grandkids. It's the kind of go-all-out attitude he had in his coaching days. "One thing I taught them was that you can be the best of friends, but when you play sports and cross that line on the field, you're not friends anymore. When you come back off the line you're friends again. You play cards to win."

His grandfather's favorite saying was "Watch your shoes." "It meant watch where you put your shoes when you step out, so you don't get in trouble," Gerald explained.

I asked Gerald to reflect on the changes he has seen over the years. "Working in a steel mill town, on Sundays you'd put clean clothes on, go to church, have a family dinner. It was a change of pace. It's very irritating to me today when I see somebody coming to church looking like slobs. I think you should have some value and respect, not only for yourself but for the Church. I still believe to this day that you should go to church every Sunday and listen to the gospel. Listen to what the priest has to say. There's always value to help everybody."

He believes in the value of families sitting down to dinner like they used to do. "We sat down at dinner every day, and that's why the children have a close relationship with my wife—because they would talk about things."

Self-sufficiency. Responsibility. Politeness. Family values. Respect for the Church. Old world values that should still have a firm place in today's world.

Chapter 11

From One Dedicated Dad to Another

What's it like to have an involved father, someone who's a role model, who instills the right kind of values in a son? How much of a difference does it make in an individual's life? Does it help a son become a good father himself?

Someone who is fortunate to know the answers to those questions is my husband, Jerry, whose dad, Gerald, is a wonderful example. There were so many different ways in which Gerald exemplified everything you'd want to see in a caring, loving dad who guides his son on the right path. Let's dig deep into some of them.

Family First

"My dad went to work early and came home early, so he was always involved in what we were doing. We went everywhere with him," says Jerry, who has two older sisters, Karen and Cindy, and a younger brother, Matt. "I remember asking him where he was going and he'd say, 'I'm going to see a man about a dog.' It was his standard answer."

His dad wouldn't reveal the errand or the destination, but in effect, he was saying the kids could tag along to find out.

And even if they just went to the grocery store, he always made it fun. Going everywhere with his dad meant Jerry would be placed in situations where it was natural to interact with people of all ages and backgrounds and where you might just have to use your imagination and figure out how to have fun. "It was as normal as waking up in the morning, brushing your teeth, and making your bed. What you realize over time is that experience drives the bus," he says.

Sporting Bonds

The family was very active in all kinds of sports. Karen was in dance and pageants and Cindy was a preeminent gymnast. It meant that Jerry spent hours and even days at their events watching them participate for a few minutes and then finding ways to entertain himself during the remainder of the event. "You don't realize it as a kid, but it broadens your horizon and the way you look at things."

His father's sport was softball. Jerry kept score and interacted with everyone. "The adults would sit around and socialize after the game, and my buddies and I would hit balls in the playground." In Jerry's case, baseball was the sport in which he flourished at a young age. "My dad would say there were two constants that you needed in baseball: defense and speed. You don't know what's going to happen with hitting and pitching. You hope you get a hit. You hope the pitcher can pitch. Our constants were family, church, and sports."

His dad's advice to Jerry was that while he was good, if he wanted to improve his game, he needed to play with better players than his friends and move up a level. Jerry balked at the idea. His dad's approach was not to force the issue. "He'd say, 'I'm not going to tell you what to do. I'm telling you, here's the opportunity if you want it.' That was the thing about my dad. He would never tell you to do something. He would just present it as an option. Here are the facts. Do what you want with them. If you want to get better, you have to play with different guys." That's what Jerry did, and he says it made him a better player.

When he was a freshman at DeMatha high school, he got cut from the baseball team. His dad told him to work hard and try again the next year. So Jerry played on two baseball teams during the summer, made the JV team, and eventually made the varsity team. In his senior year, he was captain of his team, First Team All WMAC, honorable mention all MET, and defensive MVP. "What my dad applauded was the journey I took to get those titles. Following that example is what will allow you to prosper in life. He crystallized that for me."

Social Stimulus

Jerry's family was very social. His mom and dad threw an annual crab feast for as many as three hundred people and gathered a similar size crowd for his sisters' high school graduation parties. At these events, his dad always had jobs for them, such as putting ice in the cooler and getting buns for the grill. "You never felt like you were just a kid in this scenario. You were a kid that had responsibilities," he said, jokingly. "I think the attitude was to keep the kids busy to keep them out of trouble."

Jerry's dad tailgated at every Redskins game, even when the team was not enjoying success. "Even when the Redskins were terrible, he would have as many as fifty people at his tailgate. He always found a way to bring people together, and now that's what we're teaching our kids through Truman Charities."

Jerry believes that observing his dad host the parties was great training for the Truman Charities events we hold four or five times a year. "I know how to run one-hundred-person parties from watching my dad hold events and tailgates . . . create a checklist, delegate some of the activities, that kind of thing. It becomes second nature, like any other discipline you might have." And practice makes perfect. "It's just something that you do, and you keep doing it to try to make it better each time."

Work Ethic

"Dad always taught us to work hard, do our best, and give it our all," Jerry said. "He would tell us never do a half-assed job. Whatever you're doing, finish it and do it right. That's a life changer. You don't just wake up one morning with a work ethic."

There were always jobs to do around the house, which instilled a sense of responsibility and family cohesiveness. It was a 'take out the trash first, do your job, and then go have fun' environment. "You had to understand it was bigger than the individual. If somebody's going rogue, you're dragging the whole family with you. And you have to respect that. I didn't get where I am because I just showed up. It's because of the work ethic Dad and Mom instilled in me."

When Jerry started cutting grass in third grade, he made good money—twenty dollars a month and as much as eighty dollars a week in the summer. His dad always encouraged him to save his earnings for a rainy day. "That was the best possible thing to teach a child. You'd never really have a rainy day. If it rained, it wouldn't be so bad because you'd saved money for it. I took that to heart and taught it to my own kids."

Church Influence

The Catholic faith was important in the Truman household. Jerry and Matt were both altar boys. The family went to mass together Sunday mornings or sometimes at 5:30 p.m. on a Saturday. "We were always early. The Sunday morning routine was to take a shower, brush your teeth, get dressed—and no jeans, no shorts—have breakfast, and go to church." They were always twenty minutes early.

"It wasn't just the spiritual part. It was spending an hour as a family unit, not watching TV or on your phone, and not talking, just listening. Even if you weren't praying or thinking about God, that ability to reflect on what you were doing and doing it together as a family was an invaluable asset to your happiness. Dad always said you have two ears and a mouth for a reason. Listen twice as much as you talk."

Discipline and Respect

Jerry says that although his dad was a great motivator, he was also a disciplinarian, and there were things that weren't up for debate. First and foremost was having respect for his mom.

"I learned the hard way. I said something to her that wasn't so nice, and no sooner were the words out of my mouth than he popped me in the mouth. I went down and got back up bleeding. No words were ever said, and that's the only time he ever got truly physical with me. But you knew where the line was, and I never crossed it again." His dad not only insisted on respect for one's parents but also for the church community, and for one's elders. "Don't just think about yourself," was the message, Jerry said.

Sage Advice

Jerry's dad's way of counseling was vividly on display when Jerry embarked on his career. Fresh out of school, Jerry earned a good salary working at a bank. But he had an opportunity to become an investment advisor, which was commission-based.

"I asked my dad for advice, and he said, 'When I was your age, I had two daughters and was living in an apartment. What decision would you have made?'" Jerry told his dad he'd have taken the path of security, and his dad asked him to think about his own situation. Jerry was single and without family responsibilities at the time. "Basically, he was saying, 'Hey dummy. You got nothing to lose.' Instead of telling you what to think, he was teaching you how to think, how to formulate your thoughts."

The Next Generation

Jerry's dad continues to be a mentor, treating his grandkids the way he treated Jerry. Jerry remembers standing next to him while he worked on cars and handing wrenches to him.

"I didn't know what I was doing, and I didn't have any real interest in working on the car. But I did it because he loved doing it. I'm not interested in ripping out a transmission and rebuilding, but I certainly have a love for classic cars and fast cars. So that's instilled in the boys as well. Dad was driving us in his GT convertible the other day and the kids were thrilled. My dad loved cars, so we all loved cars."

Lessons Learned

Jerry stressed the importance of family. His dad worked for the government and his mom was a homemaker. "They didn't have an inordinate amount of money, but they found ways for us to have fun. The bottom line is, they would always make it work. You have to work, you have to eat, you have to take care of clients in your business, but when there's family time, it should be family time. Try to keep the home a peaceful, happy, fun place where there's respect. Family is the most important thing."

I asked Jerry what advice he would give young men growing up without the benefit of a father in the home. "Find a mentor wherever you can," he said. "There are people out there willing to help. People are compassionate and caring. You just have to give them the opportunity." And be persistent. Don't give up. "If someone says no, go to the next person."

Jerry's final thought honors his father's influence. "If my dad wasn't in the picture, there's no way I would be the person I am now."

Chapter 12

A Call to Fathers:
You are Wanted, Needed,
and Loved

The relationship with your father is precious and begins the day you are born, with your very first breath. It's a foundational aspect of life, and it's important to note that it's value is equal to that of the relationship with your mother.

Each parent brings a unique set of traits that help a child feel safe, secure, and loved throughout their childhood. What has become clear to me after conducting the extensive interviews in this book and undertaking additional scientific research is that an absent father, for whatever reason, leaves the mother facing an arduous task: striving to be two people to compensate for an irreplaceable presence.

As we have seen, the void left by an absent father can lead to a myriad of challenges including poor academic performance, increased alcohol and drugs addiction, becoming a victim of sex trafficking, homelessness, and even suicide.

As David Blankenhorn, founder and president of the Institute for American Values, codirector of The Marriage Opportunity Council, and author of *Fatherless America* says, "Fatherlessness is the leading cause of declining child well-being in our society. It is also the engine driving our most urgent social problems." He goes on to say that despite this, it is frequently ignored as a problem.

And expert David Popenoe points out, "Almost anything bad that can happen to a child occurs with much greater frequency to the children of divorce and those who live in single-parent families. Strong families with involved fathers in lifelong marriages are irreplaceable for a strong and stable moral order, for adult wellbeing, and ultimately for the wellbeing and success in life of their children. If we continue down the path of fatherlessness, we are headed for social disaster. In the final analysis, every father counts."

Jack Brewer of the nonprofit America First Policy Institute appeals for an all-out pro-fatherhood messaging campaign from athletes, celebrities, musicians, actors, and national role models. "To address this crisis, we must first speak openly about the problem of fatherless children. Then, we must focus on fixing it by promoting strong families, confronting cultural malaise, and sharing the joys of fatherhood. It is a tall task but a worthwhile one. AFPI believes it is time for a new vision for American families. The costs of broken homes and father-lessness have plagued society, and today we are reaping the effects."

All of these expert voices resoundingly speak to encourage young men to understand the impact and value they hold within society, especially the need to handle the daunting prospect of becoming fathers themselves when they have not had the benefit of positive paternal figures. I can only imagine how scary it must be for young men to consider fatherhood when they have no idea what being a good father looks like. My challenge to them is to have faith in nature. Have faith that when you hold your newborn son or daughter, an overwhelming profound feeling of love and purpose will envelop you, turning apprehension into confidence and joy.

My personal experience reinforces this belief. Witnessing the moment my husband cradled our sons for the first time was nothing short of miraculous. I saw the instant transformation as he lovingly looked into their eyes, an unspoken vow to be their guardian and protector. I knew, there and then, he would die for our children if needed. Those were moments etched in my heart forever, moments I will treasure all my life.

Imagine the joy of being able to give the gift of a warm and loving home to your children, where they are emboldened to explore and take risks, secure in the knowledge that their parents are a constant, unwavering source of support and guidance. A home where you provide them the courage to go out and take chances in the world knowing that when life throws them curveballs, both mother and father are there to pick up the pieces and give them the love and support they need to go out and try again.

Your family's legacy can start with you. The absence of a father in your own life may make your journey more difficult, but it does not make it impossible. You have the strength to not only become a strong leader but also become an amazing father.

Take heart in knowing that:

- You are more than a potential father. You are a catalyst for change.

- You are not only a figure of authority. You are a source of comfort and guidance.

- You are not only a role model, you are also an architect of your child's future.

- You are not simply a disciplinarian. You are a provider of wisdom and guidance.

- You are not only a partner in parenting, you are also an irreplaceable half of a whole.

If there is only one takeaway I would like young men to get from this book, it is this:

You are not only wanted,

You are needed.

But most importantly,

You are LOVED.

Acknowledgments

I would like to thank my mother, who sacrificed immensely to do what was best for us; Jerry, who showed me what a loving husband and father looks like; and my boys. The three of you were the inspiration for creating the podcast series and book.

To everyone who agreed to be a part of this podcast series and book, thank you. I know how hard it is to relive some parts of your past. I want you to know how much each one of your stories will help so many children. Your bravery and selflessness are inspirational. And Malcolm, I want to thank you for helping me put all my thoughts and interviews into a beautifully written book.

Notes

1. The Fatherhood Factor

Sarah M. Allen and Kerry J. Daly, "The effects of father involvement: An updated research summary of the evidence," University of Guelph Centre for Families, Work and Well-Being, 2007, https://search.worldcat.org/ title/ effects-of-father-involvement-an-updated-research-summary-of-the-evidence/oclc/225639215.

Dionne Barnes-Proby, Celia J. Gomez, Monica Williams, Matt Strawn, and Isabel Leamon, "Programs for Incarcerated Parents: Preliminary Findings from a Pilot Survey," Santa Monica, CA: RAND Corporation, 2022, https://www.rand.org/pubs/research_reports/RRA1412-1.html.

Stephen Baskerville, "The Fatherhood Crisis: Time for a New Look?" National Center for Policy Analysis, June 30, 2002, https://www.ncpathinktank.org/pub/st267?pg=3.

Deirdre Bell, "The Importance of Dads," Boba, April 18, 2017, https://boba.com/blogs/boba-reads/the-importance-of-dads.

Henry B. Biller and Richard S. Solomon, *Child Maltreatment and Paternal Deprivation: A Manifesto for Research, Prevention, and Treatment,* (Lexington, MA: Lexington Books, 1986.)

Henry Biller, *Paternal Deprivation: Family School, Sexuality, and Society,* (Lexington, MA: Lexington Books, 1974.)

N. Cabrera, H. E. Fitzgerald, R.H. Bradley, and L. Roggman, "Modeling the dynamics of paternal influences on children over the life course," *Applied Developmental Science,* 2007;11(4):185-189.

"Children's Living Arrangements: Children Under 18 Years and Marital Status of Parents by Age of The Child: 2007 and 2023," US Census Bureau, November 14, 2023, https://www.census.gov/library/visualizations/interactive/childrens-living-arrangements.html.

K. Alison Clarke-Stewart, "And Daddy makes three: The father's impact on mother and young Child," *Child Development,* 49(2), 466–478, https://doi.org/10.2307/1128712K.

K. Alison Clarke-Stewart, "The Father's contribution," in *The Father-Infant Relationship: Observational Studies in the Family Setting,* ed. F. Pedersen, (New York: Praeger, 1980).

E. M. Cummings and A. W. O'Reilly, "Fathers in family context: Effects of marital quality on child adjustment," in M. E. Lamb (Ed.), *The role of the father in child development,* ed M. E. Lamb, (New York: Wiley, 1997.)

Juan Del Toro, Adam Fine, and Ming-Te Wang, "The intergenerational effects of paternal incarceration on children's social and psychological well-being from early childhood to adolescence," *Development and psychopathology,* 35(2), 558–569, May 2023, https://doi.org/10.1017/S0954579421001693.

K. Erlandsson, A. Dsilna, I. Fagerberg, and K. Christensson, "Skin-to-skin care with the father after cesarean birth and its effect on newborn crying and prefeeding behavior," in *Birth* (Berkeley, Calif., 2007), 34(2), 105–114. https://doi.org/10.1111/j.1523-536X.2007.00162.x.

"Family Structure and Children's Living Arrangements 2012,"
Current Population Report, US Census Bureau, July 1, 2012.

Warren Farrell and John Gray, *The Boy Crisis,* (Dallas:
Benbella Books, 2018.)

Kenneth W. Griffin, Gilbert J. Botvin, Lawrence M. Scheier,
Tracy Diaz, and Nicole L. Miller, "Parenting Practices as
Predictors of Substance Use, Delinquency, and Aggression
Among Urban Minority Youth: Moderating Effects of
Family Structure and Gender," *Psychology of Addictive
Behaviors* 14, June 2000, 174-184.

"Health Care for Homeless Women," Committee on Health
Care for Underserved Women, The American College of
Gynecologists and Obstetricians, October 2013,
https://www.acog.org/clinical/clinical-guidance/commitee-
opinion/articles/2013/10/health-care-for-homeless-women.

"Historical Living Arrangements of Children," US Census
Bureau, November 2023, https://www.census.gov/data/
tables/time-series/demo/families/children.html.

"Information on Poverty and Income Statistics: A Summary of
2012 Current Population Survey Data," https://aspe.hhs.gov/
reports/information-poverty-income-statistics-summary-
2012-current-population-survey-data-0.

Doris J. James, "Profile of Jail Inmates, 2002," Bureau of Justice
Statistics Special Report, Department of Justice, Office of
Justice Programs, July 2004, https://bjs.ojp.gov/content/pub/
pdf/pji02.pdf.

R. Jia, L. E. Kotila, and S. J. Schoppe-Sullivan, "Transactional
relations between father involvement and preschoolers'

socioemotional adjustment," *Journal of Family Psychology,* 2012, https://doi.org/10.1037/a0030245.

Melissa S. Kearney, "The Explosive Rise of Single-Parent Families Is Not a Good Thing," *New York Times,* September 17, 2023, https://www.nytimes.com/2023/09/17/opinion/single-parent families-income-inequality-college.html.

Melissa S. Kearney, *The Two-Parent Privilege: How Americans Stopped Getting Married and Started Falling Behind,* (Chicago: University of Chicago Press, 2023.)

Raymond A. Knight and Robert A. Prentky, "The Developmental Antecedents of Adult Adaptions of Rapist Sub-types," *Criminal Justice and Behavior,* 14, no. 4 (1987): 413-14.

Chris Knoester and Dana L. Haynie, "Community Context, Social Integration into Family, and Youth Violence," *Journal of Marriage and Family* 67, no 3 (2005): 767-80.

Richard Koestner, C. Franz, and J. Weinberger, "The Family Origins of Empathic Concerns: A Twenty-Six-Year Longitudinal Study," *Journal of Personality and Social Psychology* 58, no 4 (April 1990): 709-17.

Stephanie Kramer, "U.S. has world's highest rate of children living in single-parent households," Pew Research Center, December 12, 2019, https://www.pewresearch.org/short-reads/2019/12/12/u-s-children-more-likely-than-children-in-other-countries-to-live-with-just-one-parent/.

Sheila Fitzgerald Krein and A. Beller, "Educational Attainment of Children from Single-Parent Families: Differences by Exposure, Gender, and Race," *Demography* 25 (May 1988): 403-26.

"Living Arrangements of Children under 18 Years and Marital Status of Parents by Age, Sex, Race, and Hispanic Origin/2 and Selected Characteristics of the Child for all Children 2010," US Census Bureau, Census.gov.

D. Manning and K. A. Lamb, "Adolescent well-being in cohabiting, married, and single-parent families," *Journal of Marriage & Family,* 65, 876-893.

Sara McLanahan and Gary Sandefur, *Growing Up with a Single Parent,* (Cambridge: Harvard University Press, 1997.)

Clare Morell, "Fathers Matter," *National Review,* June 20, 2021, https://www.nationalreview.com/2021/06/fathers-matter/.

Christine Winquist Nord and Jerry West, "Fathers' and Mothers' Involvement in Their Children's Schools by Family Type and Resident Status, (NCES 2001-032). Washington, D.C.: U.S. Department of Education, National Center for Education Statistics, 2001.

S. Nugent, "Cultural and psychological influences on the father's role in infant development," *Journal of Marriage and the Family,* 1991;53:475-485.

F. A. Pedersen and R. L. Kain, "Parent-infant and husband wife interactions observed at age five months," in *The Father-Infant Relationship: Observational Studies in the Family Setting,* ed F. Pedersen (New York: Praeger, 1980), 71-86.

David Popenoe, *Families without Fathers: Fatherhood, Marriage and Children in American Society,* (New York: Routledge, 2009.)

Cesar J. Rebellon, "Reconsidering the Broken Homes/ Delinquency Relationship and Exploring Its Mediating Mechanism (S)," *Criminology* 40(1):103–36.

Rochester Area Fatherhood Network, http://www.rochester-areafatherhoodnetwork.org/statistics.

R. P. Rohner and R. A. Veneziano, (2001), "The importance of father love: History and contemporary evidence," *Review of General Psychology*, 5, (4), 382-405.

Jeffrey Rosenberg and W. Bradford Wilcox, "The importance of fathers in the healthy development of children," US Department of Health and Human Services, Administration for Children and Families Administration on Children, Youth and Families, Children's Bureau, Office on Child Abuse and Neglect, 2006, https://cantasd.acf.hhs.gov/wp-content/uploads/Importance-of-Fathers-Healthy-Development.pdf.

Flory Louis Perone Seidel, "The Proclivity of Juvenile Crime in Fatherless Homes: an Urban Perspective," University of Arizona Global Campus ProQuest Dissertations Publishing, https://www.proquest.com/docview/2628794018?pq-origsite=gscholar&fromopenview=true.

US Department of Justice, "What Can the Federal Government Do to Decrease Crime and Revitalize Communities?" Panel Papers, Office of Justice Programs, National Institute of Justice, 1998, 11 https://www.ncjrs.gov/pdffiles/172210.pdf.

"Why Absent Fathers Harm Children and Ruin Society," Academy of Ideas, August 14, 2023, https://academyofideas.com/2023/08/why-absent-fathers-harm-children-and-ruin-society/.

2. My Story

Justine Carbery, "The Importance of the Father-Daughter Relationship," The Gloss, https://thegloss.ie/father-daughter-relationship/.

"Dads Make the Difference," Institute for Shelter Care, https://instituteforsheltercare.org/dadsmakethedifference/.

"FACT SHEET: Fathers Matter – Pass It On," America First Policy Institute, https://americafirstpolicy.com/latest/fact-sheet-fathers-matter-pass-it-on.

Lisa Kindleberger Hagan and Janet Kuebli, "Mothers' and fathers' socialization of preschoolers' physical risk taking," *Journal of Applied Developmental Psychology,* 28(1):2-14, https://www.researchgate.net/publication/223230775_Mothers'_and_fathers'_socialization_of_preschoolers'_physical_risk_taking.

Brett and Kate McKay, "5 Ways Fathers Hugely Influence Their Daughters," Art of Manliness, October 2, 2023, https://www. artofmanliness.com/people/fatherhood/5-ways-fathers-hugely-influence-on-their-daughters/.

Clare Morell, "Fathers Matter," *National Review,* June 20, 2021, https://www.nationalreview.com/2021/06/fathers-matter/.

Linda Nielsen, *Father-Daughter Relationships: Contemporary Research and Issues*, (New York: Routledge, 2019.)

Erin Pougnet, Lisa A. Serbin, Dale M. Stack, Jane E. Ledingham, and Alex E. Schwartzman, "The Intergenerational Continuity of Fathers' Absence in a Socioeconomically Disadvantaged Sample," *Journal of Marriage and Family* 74, no. 3 (2012): 540–55, http://www.jstor.org/stable/41507290.

Rochester Area Fatherhood Network, http://www.rochester
areafatherhoodnetwork.org/statistics.

R. P. Rohner and R. A. Veneziano, "The importance of father
love: History and contemporary evidence," *Review of
General Psychology*, 5, (4), 382-405.

J. Rosenberg and W. B. Wilcox, "The importance of fathers in
the healthy development of children," US Department of
Health and Human Services, Administration for Children
and Families Administration on Children, Youth and
Families, Children's Bureau, Office on Child Abuse and
Neglect, 2006.

Ali Serdar Sağkal, Yalçın Özdemir, and Nermin Koruklu,
"Direct and indirect effects of father-daughter relationship on
adolescent girls' psychological outcomes: The role of
basic psychological need satisfaction," *Journal of Adolescence,*
2018 Oct:68:32-39. doi: 10.1016/j.adolescence.2018.07.001.

A. Sarkadi, R. Kristiansson, F. Oberklaid and S. Bremberg,
"Fathers' involvement and children's developmental
outcomes: a systematic review of longitudinal studies,"
Acta Paediatrica (Oslo, Norway: 1992), 97(2), 153–158.
doi:10.1111/j.1651-2227.2007.00572.x.

D. Scott Sibley and Katie Granger, "How Fathers Influence
Their Daughters Romantic Relationships," Institute for
Family Studies, July 15, 2019, https://ifstudies.org/blog/
how-fathers-influence-their-daughters-romantic-
relationships.

"The Trauma of Children of People with Addiction,"
Psych Central, https://psychcentral.com/lib/the-trauma-
of-children-of-addicts-and-alcoholics.

3. How Everclear's Art Alexakis Overcame Darkness

Carmen Noemi Velez and Patricia Cohen, "Suicidal Behavior and Ideation in a Community Sample of Children: Maternal and Youth Reports," *Journal of the American Academy of Child and Adolescent Psychiatry* 273, (1988): 349-56.

Gavin Edwards, "Clear Unpleasant Danger," Details magazine, May 1996, https://whitelightning.org/thepress/de9605.htm.

J. Elliot, "Art Alexis of Everclear at The Vogue," December 8, 2019, https://thevogue.com/artists/art-alexakis/.

C. W. Kienhorst, E. J. de Wilde, J. Van den Bout, R. F. Diekstra, and W. H. Wolters, "Characteristics of suicide attempters in a population-based sample of Dutch adolescents," *British Journal of Psychiatry,* 156, 243-248.

G. R. Weitoft, H. Anders, B. Haglund, and M. Rosen, "Mortality, severe morbidity, and injury in children living with single parents in Sweden: a population-based study," *Lancet* 361, 289–295.

Cicero Wilson, "What Can the Federal Government Do To Decrease Crime and Revitalize Communities," January 5-7, 1998, NIJ Research Frum, US Department of Justice, https://www.ojp.gov/pdffiles/172210.pdf.

4. Chef Al's Recipe for Recovery

"CASA 1999 teen/parent drug survey reveals: dads awol in teen substance abuse battle," The National Center on Addiction and Substance Abuse at Columbia University, http://www.fact.on.ca/newpaper/co990830.htm.

"FACT SHEET: Fatherhood and Crime," America First Policy Institute, https://americafirstpolicy.com/issues/fact-sheet-fatherhood-and-crime#.

"Fatherless Epidemic," National Center for Fathering, 2015, https://fathers.com/wp39/wp-content/uploads/2015/07/fatherlessInfographic.pdf.

David Hagedorn, "Childhood trauma. Drugs. Alcohol. A chef who chose recovery hopes his story can help others," *Washington Post,* February 5, 2019, https://www.washingtonpost.com/lifestyle/food/childhood-trauma-drugs-alcohol-a-chef-who-chose-recovery-hopes-his-story-can-help-others/2019/02/04/3c5f6c5a-232b-11e9-ad53-824486280311_story.html.

J. M. Solis, J. M. Shadur, A. R. Burns, and A. M. Hussong, "Understanding the diverse needs of children whose parents abuse substances," *Current drug abuse reviews,* 5(2), 135–147. https://doi.org/10.2174/1874473711205020135.

Shabeer Syed, Ruth Gilbert, and Miranda Wolpert, "Parental Alcohol Misuse and the Impact on Children: A Rapid Evidence Review of Service Presentations and Interventions," Children's Policy Research Unit, 2018, DOI:10.13140/RG.2.2.31073.97123.

"The Trauma of Children of People with Addiction," Psych Central, https://psychcentral.com/lib/the-trauma-of-children-of-addicts-and-alcoholics.

5. From Abuse to Hope

"Effects of domestic violence on children," US Department of Health and Human Services, Office on Women's Health, https://www.womenshealth.gov/relationships-and-safety/domestic-violence/effects-domestic-violence-children.

"Fast Facts: Preventing Child Abuse & Neglect," Centers for Disease Control and Prevention, https://www.cdc.gov/violenceprevention/childabuseandneglect/fastfact.html.

R. McDonald, E. N. Jouriles, S. Ramisetty-Mikler, R. Caetano, and C. E. Green, "Estimating the Number of American Children Living in Partner-Violent Families," *Journal of Family Psychology,* 20(1): 137-142.

S. M. Monnat and R. F. Chandler, "Long Term Physical Health Consequences of Adverse Childhood Experiences," *The Sociologist Quarterly,* 56(4): 723-752.

The Victor Marx Story and Testimony, https://www.youtube.com/watch?v=cVLnO1YI0-g.

L. Vargas, J. Cataldo, and S. Dickson, "Domestic Violence and Children," in G.R. Walz & R.K. Yep (Eds.), VISTAS: *Compelling Perspectives on Counseling,* 67-69, (Alexandria, VA: American Counseling Association).

Victor Marx/All Things Possible Ministries website, https://victormarx.com.

6. Beyond Sex Trafficking

"America's Families and Living Arrangements: 2022," US Census Bureau (2022), https://www.census.gov/data/tables/2022/demo/families/cps-2022.html.

Jeanne L. Allert, "Domestic Minor Familial Sex Trafficking: A National Study of Prevalence, Characteristics, and Challenges across the Justice Process," Institute for Shelter Care, 2022, https://instituteforsheltercare.org/familial/.

Lydia Anderson, Chanell Washington, Rose M. Kreider and Thomas Gryn, "Home Alone: More Than A Quarter of All Households Have One Person," United States Census Bureau, June 8, 2023, https://www.census.gov/library/stories/2023/06/more-than-a-quarter-all-households-have-one-person.html#.

Nada Hassanein, "When foster care kids are sex trafficked, some states fail to figure it out," *USA Today,* November 25, 2023, https://www.usatoday.com/story/news/nation/2023/11/25/states-fail- foster-care-kids-sex-trafficked/71679922007/.

Krystal Clear Foundation, www.krystalclearfoundation.org.

Clare Morell, "Fathers Matter," *National Review,* June 20, 2021, https://www.nationalreview.com/2021/06/fathers-matter/.

"Protecting Your Children from Human Trafficking," https://www.empowerhernetwork.org/2023/01/31/protecting-your-children-from-human-trafficking/.

"Reducing recidivism by breaking bonds of attachment to traffickers and 'The Game' lifestyle," https://endingthe-game.com.

Melissa Fletcher Stoeltie, "Child sex trafficking a huge problem in Texas and the nation," mysantonio.com, July 17, 2012, https://mysanantonio.com/news/local/child-sex-trafficking-a-huge-problem-in-texas-and-3714153.php.

Rachel Swaner, Melissa Labriola, Michael Rempel, Allyson Walker, and Joseph Spadafore, "Youth Involvement in the Sex Trade: A National Study," Center for Court Innovation, March 2016, htps://www.ojp.gov/pdffiles1/ojjdp/grants/249952.pdf.

"Understanding Human Trafficking," Polaris Project, https://polarisproject.org/understanding-human-trafficking/.

Emma Waters, "U.S.A. Is a Top Destination for Child Sex Trafficking, and It's Happening in Your Neighborhood," The Heritage Foundation, July 27, 2023, https://www.heritage. org/crime-and-justice/commentary/us-top-destination-child-sex-trafficking-and-its-happening-your.

"Why So Young? – Why the average age a child is first exploited through prostitution is 13," Shared Hope International, March 11, 2011, https://sharedhope.org/2011/03/11/why-so-young-why-the-average-age-a-child-is-first-exploited-through-prostitution-is-13/.

7. When Stepdads Step Up: NFL Player Justin Pugh's Story

D. A. Brent, N. M. Melhem, A. S. Masten, G. Porta, and M. W. Payne, "Longitudinal effects of parental bereavement on adolescent developmental competence," *Journal of Clinical Child and Adolescent Psychiatry,* 2012;41(6):778–91. doi:10.1080/15374416.2012.717871.

J. A. Cohen, A. P. Mannarino, and K. Knudsen, "Treating childhood traumatic grief: a pilot study," *Journal of Clinical Child and Adolescent Psychiatry,* 2004;43(10): 1225–33, doi:10.1097/01.chi.0000135620.15522.38.

"Father's death does not affect growth and maturation but hinders reproduction: evidence from adolescent girls in post-war Estonia," *Biology Letters,* 2015, https://royalsocietypublishing.org/doi/10.1098/rsbl.2015.0752.

L. B. Gray, R. A. Weller, M. Fristad, and E. B. Weller, "Depression in children and adolescents two months after the death of a parent," *Journal of Affective Disorders,* 2011;135(1–3):277–83, doi:10.1016/j.jad.2011.08.009.

M. B. Guldin, J. Li, H. S. Pedersen, C. Obel, E. Agerbo, M. Gissler, et al., "Incidence of suicide among persons who had a parent who died during their childhood: a population-based cohort study," *JAMA Psychiatry,* 2015;72(12):1227–34, doi:10.1001/jamapsychiatry. 2015.2094.

Paul Hemez and Chanell Washington, "Number of Children Living Only With Their Mothers Has Doubled in Past 50 Years," United States Census Bureau, https://www.census.gov/ library/stories/2021/04/number-of-children-living-only-with-their-mothers-has-doubled-in-past-50-years.html.

O. M. Kwok, R. A. Haine, I. N. Sandler, T. S. Ayers, S. A. Wolchik, and J. Y. Tein, "Positive parenting as a mediator of the relations between parental psychological distress and mental health problems of parentally bereaved children," *Journal of Clinical Child and Adolescent Psychiatry,* 2005;34(2):260–71. doi:10.1207/s15374424jccp3402_5.

J. Li, M. Vestergaard, S. Cnattingius, M. Gissler, B. H. Bech, C. Obel, et al. "Mortality after parental death in childhood: a Nationwide cohort study from three Nordic countries," *PLoS Medicine,* 2014;11(7) doi:10.1371/journal.pmed. 1001679.

"New 2021 Data Visualization Shows Parent Mortality: 44.2% Had Lost at Least One Parent," US Census Bureau, March 21, 2023, https://www.census.gov/library/ stories/2023/03/losing-our-parents.html.

A. Nickerson, R. A. Bryant, I. M. Aderka, D. E. Hinton, and S. G. Hofmann, "The impacts of parental loss and adverse parenting on mental health: findings from the National Comorbidity Survey-Replication," *Psychological Trauma-Theory Research Practice and Policy*, 2013;5(2):119–27, doi:10.1037/A0025695.

Steven Pham, Giovanna Porta, Candice Biernesser, Monica Walker Payne, Satish Iyengar, Nadine Melhem, and David A. Brent, "The Burden of Bereavement: Early-Onset Depression and Impairment in Youths Bereaved by Sudden Parental Death in a 7-Year Prospective Study," *American Journal of Psychiatry*, 175(9):887-896.

David Popenoe, *Families without Fathers: Fatherhood, Marriage and Children in American Society*, 2009, (New York: Routledge, 2009).

Y. Stikkelbroek, D. H. Bodden, E. Reitz, et al, "Mental health of adolescents before and after the death of a parent or sibling," *European Child and Adolescent Psychiatry* 25, 49–59 (2016). https://doi.org/10.1007/s00787-015-0695-3.

"Why Absent Fathers Harm Children and Ruin Society," Academy of Ideas, August 14, 2023, https://academyofideas.com/2023/08/why-absent-fathers-harm-children-and-ruin-society/.

J. W. Worden and P. R. Silverman, "Parental death and the adjustment of school-age children," *OMEGA - Journal of Death and Dying*, 1996; 33(2):91–102. doi:10.2190/P77L-F6F6-5W06-NHBX.

9. From Cult Victim to Loving Father of Three

Sam Jahara, "The Psychological Impact on Children who Grow Up in Cults," Brighton and Hove Psychotherapy, August 6, 2023, https://www.brightonandhovepsychotherapy.com/

blog/the-psychological-impact-on-children-who-grow-up-in-cults/#.

Hunter Levitan, Eliza Thompson, and Corinne Sullivan, "These Are the 16 Scariest Cult Stories of All Time," *Cosmopolitan,* November 3, 2021, https://www.cosmopolitan.com/entertainment/a10309417/scariest-cult-stories/.

Lisa Magdelena, "Unmasking the Aftermath: 10 Psychological and Emotional Issues Experienced by Cult Survivors," Beyondpsychub, October 31, 2023, https://www.beyond-psychub.com/emotional-issues-experienced-by-cult-survivors/.

M. Pignotti, "Helping survivors of destructive cults: Applications of Thought Field Therapy," *Traumatology,* 6(3), 201–235, https://doi.org/10.1177/153476560000600304.

"Post-Cult After Effects," Spiritual Abuse Resources, https://www.spiritualabuseresources.com/articles/post-cult-after-effects.

Lauren Zazzara, "4 Notorious Cults in American History," Heinonline Blog, October 13, 2023, https://home.heinonline.org/blog/2023/10/4-notorious-cults-in-american-history/.

10. How the Death of a Father Shapes a Son's Life

P. Böckerman, M. Haapanen, and C. Jepsen, "Early parental death and its association with children's mental and economic well-being in adulthood: a nationwide population-based register study, *Journal of Epidemiology and Community Health,* 2023;77:625-631, https://jech.bmj.com/content/77/10/625.info.

Pooja Makhijani, "At the cellular level a child's loss of a father is associated with increased stress," Princton University, Office of Communications, July 18, 2017, https://www.princeton.edu/news/2017/07/18/cellular-level-childs-loss-father-associated-increased-stress.

Steven Reinberg, "Losing a Parent is Hard. Is It Harder for Boys?" *HealthDay News,* July 31, 2023, https://www.usnews.com/news/health-news/articles/2023-07-31/losing-a-parent-is-hard-is-it-harder-for-boys.

12. A Call to Fathers: You are Wanted, Needed, and Loved

David Blankenhorn, *Fatherless America: Confronting Our Most Urgent Social Problem,* (New York: Harper Perennial, 1996).

Jack Brewer, "ISSUE BRIEF: Fatherlessness and its effects on American society," America First Policy Institute, May 15, 2023, https://americafirstpolicy.com/issues/issue-brief-fatherlessness-and-its-effects-on-american-society.

David Popenoe, *Families without Fathers: Fatherhood, Marriage and Children in American Society,* (New York: Routledge, 2009).

"Why Absent Fathers Harm Children and Ruin Society," Academy of Ideas, August 14, 2023, https://academyofideas.com/2023/08/why-absent-fathers-harm-children-and-ruin-society/.

About the Author

Jamie Truman hosts the Truman Charities podcast and is a cofounder of Truman Charities, an organization that is 100 percent volunteer based.

Truman Charities has raised almost two million dollars for several charities over the past fourteen years. The organization operates with one simple and important concept: When good people get together, great things happen.

When Jamie is not working on a podcast or a Truman Charities event, she enjoys being a wife and stay-at-home mom. She is the wife of Jerry Truman and mom to three children: stepson Zack, Dominic, and Antonio.

Voices of Change
Listen Now to the Truman Charities podcast

If you're interested in supporting worthy causes listen to the Truman Charities podcast. In each episode, I have an in-depth conversation with the founder of a noteworthy charitable group, giving you the opportunity to find a charity that resonates with you. You'll also be able to hear the interviews I conducted with everyone featured in this book.

ACCESS NOW!

www.ingramcontent.com/pod-product-compliance
Lightning Source LLC
Chambersburg PA
CBHW051205120626
46547CB00013B/1208